The Unlisted Legion

The Unlisted Legion

Part of its Witness
in the Karakoram and the Khyber

JOCK PURVES

'There's a Legion that never was 'listed,
That carries no colours or crest.
But, split in a thousand detachments,
Is breaking the road for the rest.'

THE BANNER OF TRUTH TRUST

THE BANNER OF TRUTH TRUST
3, Murrayfield Road, Edinburgh EH12 6EL
P.O. Box 621, Carlisle, Pennsylvania 17013, USA

*

© The Banner of Truth Trust, 1977
First published 1977
ISBN 0 85151 245 3

*

Set in 11 on 12pt Georgian
and printed in Great Britain by
Hazell Watson & Viney Ltd
Aylesbury, Bucks

Foreword

Everything that is written in this book about people, travels and experiences, took place during the period of a very few years on the mission field (1926–30). They were full years, it is true; but few in comparison with the long and faithful missionary years of many others. I am an admirer of missionaries of the Gospel. After half a century in missionary service, a short time of it abroad, and a longer time at home, in administration, over forty years of it with my helpmeet in the Worldwide Evangelization Crusade, and with our family of four – Jean, Morag, Elspeth, and John – serving in Christian ministry abroad and at home, one cannot but be enthusiastic in the missionary cause.

It has taken me some time to decide to set down what is in the following pages. Perhaps I should have done so before now. I have dispensed with dates thinking that the real interest would lie in the events themselves, which were all before the partition of India in 1947, except for the tragic deaths of Ronald Davies and Miriam Masih which took place during the partition struggle between Hindus and Moslems. For some years before then there were missionaries in Baltistan and Ladakh which constitute what is known as Lesser or Little Thibet. No Western Christian workers as far as we know are now permitted there. Thibet proper and Afghanistan, at that time were closed to the missionary. Thibet still is, though under a different regime, that of Chinese Communism instead of Mahayana Buddhism. There have been unpredictable changes in Afghanistan where there are now servants of the Lord, but also other Westerners whose manner of life shows them to be in as dire need of salvation as any people of Central Asia.

For many years before the partition of India in 1947 there were Christian workers in Kashmir and in the North West Frontier Province (North West Pakistan). But even today it is difficult and dangerous to openly witness for Christ on the North West Frontier.

There is most urgent need for intercession in the Name which is above every name, for the salvation of Islamic, Hindu and Buddhist peoples, many of whom are now living in our country; and we should pray for those who are dedicated to full-time service to make Christ known to them. Thousands of Moslems, Hindus and Buddhists are now in Britain, besides many nominal Christians from the Indies, and there are servants of the Lord working among these immigrants in different parts of the country. The Worldwide Evangelization Crusade has missionaries serving this need, particularly in the East Midlands, among various races of Asiatic faiths. These missionaries have all served abroad among the peoples of India, Kashmir and the Middle East.

In Germany there are also Worldwide Evangelization Crusade workers among Koreans and Turks. From printing presses at Bulstrode, Bucks, broadsheets with the Gospel go across the world with testimonies to its saving power, in English, Urdu, Bengali, French and Portuguese, often to places where the missionary himself cannot go. From the Christian Literature Crusade, with its many shops in Britain, the Americas, Europe, and various parts of the world, Christian literature is reaching many peoples, while Radio Worldwide make recording after recording to be beamed to people in their own language in various parts of the world. It is for us, the church, to make use of every modern means possible to make known to the races of mankind, the Gospel of the Lord Jesus Christ which is the power of God unto salvation to everyone who believes.

I heartily express my sincere thanks to the editorial staff of the Banner of Truth Trust for their encouragement and advice. It means a great deal to me to have a second book published by the Banner of Truth Trust, the first being 'Fair Sunshine', a combined edition of two books published by the Stirling Tract Enterprise some years before, 'Sweet Believing' and 'Fair Sunshine'. These were written because of my fervent admiration for the Covenanters and the Puritans who in the seventeenth century preserved the Gospel for us. From my earliest days of assurance of salvation I have been a reader of their writings, and have continued to be so, whenever reading their works was possible.

Many years ago I often wished that an agency would come into being to republish some of the best works of the Puritans. This has been granted in the Banner of Truth Trust. My aim at one time in life was to become a Presbyterian minister. Strangely enough the Lord called me to serve Him in an interdenominational mission.

My warm thanks to Mr and Mrs Alfred Read for the use of some interesting pictures and to Mrs Jean Hall, Sleights, Whitby, for her help, at a necessary time, in retyping the manuscript. And plentiful thanks to my wife for her advice and counsel during the time I was working at it.

The present book also contains some material first published by the Stirling Tract Enterprise under the title 'Lal Sahib.'

A short list of titles of readable books relevant to the theme of this one is appended. Many more titles could be added. Most of those listed are books which hold in reverence the unique Person of the Lord Jesus Christ, the only begotten Son of God, and the 'theopneustia', the God breathed character of the Holy Scriptures. I have omitted titles of comparative religion books which are not sympathetic to the Christian faith. One or two are of geographical and mountaineering interest. Some of the books are out of print, and can only be obtained, and with difficulty, secondhand.

Readers of Rudyard Kipling will recognise the source of the verse which has suggested the title of this book. Our adaptation of part of the first verse from 'the Lost Legion', occurred to that little band of missionary men and women, and others like them, of fifty years ago whose memory has been vividly before me as I wrote these pages.

Jock Purves.
January 1977

Contents

Contents

Illustrations

1: *Challenge tremendous*

Pir Panjal, Hindu Kush, Pamir, Himalaya, Karakoram!
Names of some of the mightiest of mountains, stirring
thought and vision to seeming inaccessible mysteries of
nature. Unclimbed snowy peaks, unknown passes, unexplored deserts of mountains, uncharted seas of ice, creep-
ing, crushing glaciers, the largest outside Antarctica!
Streams at a trickle becoming leaping mighty waters
among the mightiest in the world! Summer suns like fires
of glory, the very air all golden dried! Frosts like blocks
of ice; snows fallen and become so deep they harden to
become highroads for both man and beast, and hazardous
bridges over running waters! And sparkling nights with
sky like a vast purple cushion! A royal setting for the
moon and stars, as jewels kept by God Himself for His
own special pleasure, their radiance like silver sunshine
dressing mountain and valley as the footstool of His feet.

Samarkand, Tashkent, Bokhara, Kashgar, Khotan,
Kabul, Lhasa! Forbidden cities, buried cities, religious
cities, where men may kill the righteous to do God service; gem-studied temples; austere monasteries, giant
idols looming in their dim gloom blue domes of beauty
above the dead; towers of ancient fame; mosques with
elegant minarets from which comes the muezzin's
tuneful call to prayer; carved tracery of wood, incompar-
able; lovely jade, man-made lovelier still; literature and
painting; music in word and sound! Whose minds first
thought of these things? Whose hands fashioned them?
Yet it must be said, as time makes evident, that the ulti-
mate end of man's creation is nothingness. As one of

their own poets has said, 'Hai! Hai! The end is the end! The end is nothing!'

Azoka, Genghis Khan, Tamerlane, Nadir Shah, Babur, Jehangir, Akhbar! Savages of genius, believing that the Sky or Allah had ordained that they rule all men, bringing them light! Ravening hordes, human shambles, ghastly cairns of skulls, wasted earth with their brothers' blood crying to God from it; and now they and their empires buried deep! 'Hai! Hai!,' sang the unknown Afghan poet, 'The wind has blown their swords away!'

Camel caravans with their tinkling bells; lithe-limbed muleteams; trudging and drudging burdened ponies; yaks and zhos slow moving, sure-hooved, strong and patient, the high and narrow snowy trails littered with the smelling carcases and vulture-picked bones of their fellows. Wolves, wild horses, wild asses, and wild dogs; antelope, deer, ibex, sambhur, markhor, ghoral, lynx, snow-leopards, shrill whistling marmots, bears red and black, scrawny vultures and soaring eagles. There is a word, too, for you, from the Most High, 'Be not afraid, ye beasts of the field,' in all your groaning and travailing where your fields are rough and stony indeed.

Prince Siddartha, you who claimed to be the enlightened Gautama Buddha, your four so-dreaded omens are still here, ever here – the diseased, the aged, the dead, and the saffron-robed ascetic. The Bodhi Tree branches are yet here for you to sit beside, and in their shade for you to suppose yourself coming again to the supreme knowledge of universal cause and effect; the law of becoming and passing away; the knowledge of your four great 'truths': sorrow, the cause of sorrow, the cessation of sorrow, and the Path, the Noble Eightfold Path. You still possess the hearts and minds of many. You wrote nothing, but your devotees have told of your teaching; that existence

is unhappiness; that unhappiness is caused by selfish desire; but that there is help in the following of the Noble
Eightfold Way of right desires; right speech, clear and
truthful; right views; right ways of living, of true moral-
ity, and no taking away of life, human or animal; right
livelihood without causing ill to anyone; right effort,
patient, enduring; right recognition of the past, the present and the future; and so important, right meditation,
and onwards to Nirvana, when, 'The Dew is on the Lotus!
Rise great Sun! And Lift My Leaf and Mix Me with the
Wave! Om Mani Padme Hum! The Sunrise Comes! The
Dewdrop Slips into the Shining Sea!'

Muhammad, Arabian stranger, not now a stranger
here, nor for centuries! Your adamant demand for Islam,
or submission to the will of Allah, is the creed of millions.
Those who have taken you to be the guide of their lives
say that in you is the finality of all the prophets; that
yours is the liberating message, rational for the whole race
of man; your disciple-collected messages of the Koran the
final word until the Judgment Day.

Vishnu and Siva, and lesser gods so many! Philosophies
from the times of the 'rishi' or seer, a thousand years and
more before the life on earth of the Son of Man who is the
Son of God! What worlds of thought and action the
minds of men have created within the religion of the
Hindu! No clear system; various codes of faith, their
members held together by common birth, and life forever
revolving; caste, the Vedic literature, and inevitably,
Vishnu and Siva. The world is immaterial, the sport, the
plaything of a Being who always moves away from pur-
poseful action, a world dominated and ruled by Karma
which automatically determines another birth, according
to the merit or demerit of the previous incarnation. The
Christian who would study the 'Karmkand', the whole

body of Hindu religious ceremonies, should do so with deepening heart-desire for the salvation of the Hindu. And this must be so, always, in studies of Buddhism, Islam and the religion of the Sikhs, who, parted from the teaching of the Vedas, the Vedic literature, the Brahmin priesthood and the caste system, are the followers of Kabir and Nanak. Though the living line of the religious guides is gone there are still the Writings, the Granth Sahib, elaborately worshipped, the teachings of Guru Nanak. They tell us that 'All virtues are thine, O Lord; none is mine. There is no devotion without virtue.' But who shall endue us with virtue and power livingly to express it?

And covering much of Central Asia there is the new religion, a religion without God, yet with a man-made god whose stature is only earth-high; whose plans are vast and many, and whose efforts match his plans. Communism! Already his hammer has smashed mercilessly; already he has marvellously rebuilt; already his scythe has fiercely cut down, and he has abundantly replanted; behind his massive curtains there is much ado. About nothing? No! Much land is green that once was black, and gold that once was green. Compared with this marching might, what have mattered, relatively, the static economics of Islam and the well-meaning dreams of Buddhism? Heavy smoke from oil-refineries and the output of busy factories tell us that Karl Marx has triumphed, and that Muhammad and the Buddha have lost much of their long-held day. Villages have become towns, and towns have become cities housing hundreds of thousands. Schools, colleges and universities teem with men and women, some of them with ideas of residing in the skies, if their space programmes prosper. But there are also the little-known places of silent suffering, labour camps where detained men become mere machines. Is this the religion of the future for mankind? Far from it! It is rather to be viewed as linked with the beginning of the end.

Lands of mystery, grandeur and beauty! Peoples of charm, interest and need! And, alas, in recent years of substantial hardship! Sparsely, copies of the Book are cast as bread upon the waters, in hope of a return according to divine promise. But, in reality, few have heard the Gospel of Christ adequately preached! Because of wars and political factors, missionaries are kept mostly at the thresholds of Central Asian peoples, giving the living message to them as they come out and go in. But we know that the copies of the Scriptures, and the messengers at the doors of these lands, and their preaching of the Gospel, mean more than anyone of us can know but God Himself. And we know too, that Jesus Christ is 'Lord of all', and that to Him 'every knee shall bow'.

2: *Land of the Shalimar*

For beauty, Kashmir is a land unequalled. With massive heights in all their snowy whiteness breaking into ethereal blue, clear rock-splashing streams and deep-flowing rivers like rushing thunder between sheer canyon walls, or moving with easy flow amid banks of green and brown; with dense forests pinnacled upon steeply-sloping mountain sides; with flowers of every hue and fruit abundant, Kashmir is a garden of colour, scent and usefulness. Fine trees are plentiful, walnut, chestnut, poplar, willow, ash, elm, maple, sycamore, varied fir and pine, the beautiful chenar or plane, and the magnificent deodar or Himalayan cedar, akin to the cedar of Lebanon. Here the rhododendron is at home. And the hazel, the hawthorn, and wild-rose, though small amidst such gigantic grandeur fit exquisitely into the Edenic pattern. The wooden huts of the Kashmiris, gabled and thatched, or wood roofed, yet tumbledown in some cases, look, in the distance, like Swiss chalets, and picturesquely dot the landscape among the flowers, which appear in superb unison, to praise Him whose glory is above earth and heaven.

The meadows of Kashmir, or 'marg', as they are so finely called, are among the most wonderful flower carpets of the East. There, if anywhere, nature declares that 'Solomon in all his glory was not arrayed like one of these'. With the rolling back of the thick white blanket of winter's weaving, these flowers become a changing pageant of unbelievable beauty through their seasons. Our own well-known wild flowers are there. And there is such a galaxy of pink tulips, narcissi, white and gold crocuses, irises in all their loveliness of blues and mauves, anemones, primulas, gentians, together with the superb vividness of alpine blossoms and flowers. Our own garden favourites bloom, many of them in their original home – wallflowers, the clamtis, the orchis, balsams, columbines, sunflowers, poppies, pansies, and campanulas. On this so well-watered and well-sunned side of the Himalaya, 'The Abode of the Snow', they tell of a day that was in Eden long ago, and of a day yet to be, when day and night shall be for ever day, and when of man's dim lights, and of God's great lights, there shall never be need again.

Upon the waters float seeming bits of Paradise, the lotus spread in all the wonder of its rose-pink and white, and around it gathered the delicate yellows and whites of its attendant water-lilies, as ladies-in-waiting upon a queen. All indeed is royal. The lotus is a symbol of a power now gone from Kashmir; but just beyond, in the Thibetan ranges, where all is dry and barren, and flowers are few, 'Om Mani Padme Hum', is expressed every second of the day, 'O Jewel in the Lotus! Hail!' The prayerwheels turn the written longing of the Buddhist in young and soft yellow hands, and in hands that are old and gnarled, the water-wheels, in the rush of their swift waters, uphold for a prayerful second the ever-sacred phrase, 'Om Mani Padme Hum', and the ragged flags and pennons flutter it.

To gaze into the scented beauty of the lotus is to feel something of the Buddhist awe and wonder about the mystery of life and death. And it makes one pray the more sympathetically that the Buddhist peoples might know, that although 'No man hath seen God at any time; the only begotten Son, who is in the bosom of the Father, He hath declared Him', so that their mystic philosophies of the Eternal and eternity might become fulness of joy in knowing that the Son of God is come and that there is eternal life in Him.

Some five thousand feet above the level of the sea lie the valleys of Kashmir, and from such fair and beautiful vantage points, wherever the eye can see, majestic grandeur rises in a panorama so vast that the place seems filled with echoes of the morning stars singing together, and all the sons of God shouting for joy. The named and the nameless rise to the skies in pinnacles of ice and snow, white cliffs hovering above the earth seemingly ready to fly away. Nanga Parbat, Nubra, Kunlun, Haramukh, Kolahoi, Kajinag! And great black mountain precipices hang like buttresses for a world, while far below, in lake, river and pool, are reflected the sapphire-blue and crystal of many an awesome peak.

Man, in the midst of it all, thinking God's creative thoughts, as it were, after Him, has done well enough in

[7]

certain ways. Here are some of his lovely gardens, Shali-mar, Nishat, Nasim, and more; and his long canals, float-ing gardens, flashing fountains, and marble terraces. Here also are the ruins of grand old temples, such as Martand, with their fluted pillars and trefoil arches. But, alas, they belonged to earthly, perished and perishing gods, those of snake worship, Hinduism, Buddhism – and now to Islam. Happy and prosperous times in the history of Kashmir have been rare indeed. A buffer state it has often been, and is such today. Some of its kings and rulers have been architects, artists, engineers, and men of letters who have done well in their own dim light, only to see their worth-while work pulled down and destroyed by the merciless hands of invaders whose one aim was destruction and slaughter.

Down the great valley of Kashmir comes the Jhelum, rising from a spring of deep blue water at Vernag. To it the Emperor Jehangir asked to be carried when he was dying. Out it flows and widens into the Wular Lake, the largest lake in the sub-continent, and on to Srinagar, whose main streets are its waterways, while seven city bridges cross it. At Domel, the Jhelum and the Kishen-ganga flow side by side, the one brown and muddy from gathered deposits in its long deep valley flow; the other clear, cold and green, rushes down from the snows.

3: Our coming to the Baltis

To the north of Kashmir are frontiers of the Union of Soviet Socialist Republics, and the Republic of China, Russian Turkestan having now become part of the former, and Chinese Turkestan or Sinkiang, part of the latter. Between them and Kashmir proper are the distant Himalaya, and the Karakoram, embracing in their heights and depths the lands of Baltistan or Lesser Thibet, and Ladakh or Western Thibet. Peak after peak rises piercing the skies over vast areas, many of them still uncharted, while the great icy pillar of K2, or Mt. Godwin Austen, at 28,250 ft crowns them all. Their mighty valleys hold fearsome glaciers and rivers of ice. It all presents to man a field of unlimited geographical survey, a land remote and repellent, a savage and cruel country, and one of the wonders of the world.

Beyond the tree-clad Himalaya of Kashmir live the Baltis, the people of Baltistan. They live in their villages of flat-roofed houses; and in homes cut from the mountain sides, right up to the very snouts of the glaciers. Many of the villages are extremely difficult to reach, and food in them is always scarce. There are actually hamlets of people which can be reached only by ladders made from long willow tree trunks, and in some cases by rope ladders. The Baltis are a poor people – underfed, undernourished and suffering from diseases for which no medical or surgical help is available – a poverty-stricken and wretched, but a so-likeable people, warm of heart and kindly, a hand-to-mouth, dust-to-dust folk. Wood for fuel is very scarce. The one item of food of which there is plenty is the apricot, which can be had in its season, and is dried throughout the winter. The shells covering the kernels are used as fuel, while the kernels are eaten. Not a crust of bread is wasted.

Every leaf not eaten by the sheep and goats, that wait with quivering muzzles while their young shepherds climb the trees and shake the branches, showering the leaves to the ground, is gathered in for fuel. The Baltis have been referred to by some as dregs of humanity, and sometimes they refer to themselves as such. But that is far from being the case. They are a lovable people, and there are many fine characters among them. Rather a high percentage of them are mentally disturbed, quite a number are dumb, and comparatively few are not disfigured by goitres, the result, no doubt, of having only snow water to drink, no clouds from the Indian Ocean ever crossing the massive peaks. Bone disease is common, but there is little disease of the lungs. Ardently bigoted in their Islamic religion, any mention of the Lord Jesus Christ and His Gospel is resisted with cursing and spitting by many of them. Early in the Arctic-like morning when the whole land is lying stiff and stark in its coldness, or when the rosy tints of a summer dawn usher in a day of life-giving dry heat, the Moslem call to prayer shakes the silent solitudes, tuneful and musical, but intolerant and uncompromising: 'There is no God but Allah, and Muhammed is his prophet.' And there are no Christian missionaries there, nor have there been for a long time. One wonders when they may go again.

Jack Grant, Ernest New, Rex Bavington and myself, made our way into Lesser Thibet by way of the Deosai Plateau of Demons, and the Burji La (Burji Pass), which is around 16,500 feet above the sea, a journey of over a fortnight by foot and pony from Srinagar to Skardu,

capital of the country, and on to our mission-posts of
Doghoni and Shigar. Leaving the Munshi Bagh (Teacher
Garden), Srinagar, we crossed the Wular Lake by 'dunga'
(large wooden boat), to the small village of Bandapura,
where we were almost eaten alive by mosquitoes, but
where we had a rewarding view of Haramukh (16,872
feet).

Up we went towards Tragbal, and crossed a beautiful
Pass, the Rajdiangan, amidst fir, pine and spruce forests
where sometime later Rex Bavington saw several Himalayan bears. A day or two of travel brought us among the
Dards, in Kanzalwani and Gurais, a people distinct from
Baltis and Kashmiris. Though their dress appeared to be
mostly black, there was a unique blending of other deep
colours with it. Sometime later I stayed with them for a
time. Some of them seemed to have ideas of a Greek
ancestry traceable to the armies of Alexander the Great
who soldiered in parts of Central Asia in the fourth century B.C.

From Minamarg we were getting on well towards the
Burzil Pass (11,500) when heavy falls of snow stopped us,
though it was but early autumn. By this time we had left
all signs of human habitation and were mounting up to
the Deosai Plateau where for five days we would see
neither bush nor tree, no human abode of any kind, and
possibly not meet another fellow-human, but be surrounded by hosts of mountains cleaving the skies. Our
tents stood stark and stiff in the snow.

The Kashmiri ponymen soon let us know what they
felt about things by saying that to cross the Deosai was
not now possible, and that if we tried to do so, all of us,
men and animals alike would die. With that they tumbled
into a tent, and stayed there. The ponies had little shelter.
Our tents became like snow-houses. Hopefully waiting we

kept on praying, together and alone. More snow fell and damp mists enveloped us. Again we asked the ponymen to venture up on to the Deosai. There was no grass there, they said, and they and their ponies would die. But they added that in three days' time they were expecting sunshine, and we should move then. After a time of prayer and consideration together we felt that we should ask the men to return to Minamarg, with their ponies, a day's journey back, for shelter and protection while we remained at Burzil. But it proved unnecessary for the sun broke through the clouds with cheering warmth. Snows melted and streams began to run so that we saw the rocky face of Mother Earth again. 'But', said our helpers, 'we cannot move today!'

Next day, camp was struck, and slowly in a long line we were on the ascent to the plateau. Our worthy 'men of the horse', had gathered as much 'shing' (firewood) as possible for the five days crossing of that treeless zone. Hail lashed us for a while, but soon the sun came out, shining brightly on our steep rocky paths. Boulder-strewn streams ran here and there in the desolation where rivers take their rise, and the vulture-picked carcases of animals lay close beside the narrow trails. Marmots stood by their dens watching us and uttering their shrill and strange dog-howl whistles. The barrenness was incredible. Stony plains, boulder-littered valleys, rocky hills, almost completely grassless, and yet here and there wild flowers growing. Snowy peaks formed our horizons. We had superb views of Nanga Parbat, or 'Naked Mountain', (26,620 feet), snow-covered, glistening in the sunshine like a gigantic cone of sugar. As the days passed the going became more strenuous, as we zigzagged up and down, until it was up! up! up! At last, we stood on a bed of ice at the top of the Burji La. Away, far below us, we could

see the villages of the Baltis, in the valleys of the Karakoram.

On the Balti side of the Burji La descent was painfully
steep. The bleaching bones of animals lay among the
rocks while vultures wheeled around the nauseous remains of others. Our first Balti camp was at about 14,000
feet, and from it next day we pushed on, in cold solitude,
to the small huddle of homes called Salpura. But what a
descent! Down, down, down we came with many a jolt to
the spine, and with care, lest we dislodge rock which
might fall on man or beast on the zig-zag path below.
Unbelievably, we descended over 5,000 feet in a matter of
hours, and apart from a leg injury to Rex Bavington,
through a fall in the stony Salpura River, we reached
Skardu, all in good form.

4: *Our home in Doghoni*

From Skardu we took a three-days' journey east to Doghoni in the Shyock Valley. Our first Karakoram home we
named Bethany, though no Mary nor Martha was ever
there. But it certainly was home (or 'nangnu', as the Baltis
say) for two native-garbed, turbanned and bearded missionaries, Rex Bavington and myself, Jack Grant and
Ernest New having gone to Shigar. Iman Admi, Piyara,
Jawani and Phru Chik were, eventually, there with us
too, and many a Bible reading and prayer meeting we
had within its mudbrick walls. We rather liked the place,
though it was a den of rats, bugs, lice and fleas, which
sometimes chased us from our beds on the hard mud-

floors up to our flat mud-roof, and from there to a more restful bed on the sparsely grassed ground close by. It was rented by us from Bawa Taki, old Father Christmassy Taki, whose long white beard lost itself in the wool of his long sheepskin coat. He and his family, three generations of them, shared it with us until they built another place for themselves. They were humble and well-meaning folk, and we had no objection to their presence.

The house was rather square in shape with lower walls of heavy boulders, and thick, strong mudbricks above them. The roof was of flat, Western Thibetan type. Snow lay on it through the long hard winter, but in the warm, dry and clear air of summer we were able to pitch tents on it. No rain ever fell on them since clouds from the Indian Ocean break upon the Outer Himalaya and water the lovely vales of Katyul (Kashmir). Often we were free of deep snows in our habitable valleys, for we lived, as it were, in a surround of giant cathedrals, and these towering edifices held on to the snows, and were loth to part with them until they came tumbling down in angry avalanche, or the warmth of spring brought them down in thundering brown cataracts. When the weather was suitable we would sometimes sit up on the roof, on the short chimney stacks we had built, Rex Bavington singing Gospel songs and I accompanying him on an accordion. Balti folk liked hearing us, and gathered around to listen.

Down through a wide square opening from the roof a roughly made ladder led on to the next floor where our main rooms were situated. These we entered by small doors four feet high and two feet broad. Our heads touched the smoke-blackened rafters above, but in most Balti homes, it is impossible to stand upright; families move about inside by crawling on their hands and knees. It was a trial to us to attend to the sick in them for we were often blinded by wood smoke and had to get outside for relief. Their fires burn in the middle of the floor, and there is usually no outlet for the smoke. Our living-room, dining-room and bedroom were all one, and contained a table, and a couple of wooden chairs, one of which Rex made. We put up some shelves for our Bibles and books, laid hard grass matting on the floor, and slept there in our sheets and blankets. Rats darted about, and ran across us in the night. Rex laughingly complained that they had rather cold feet! Evil smelling bugs, flat and red, dropped down on us from the rafters, and from the dusty willow branches interwoven between them, giving us sharp bites like electric jabs. Below us, underground really, and reached by a sloping tunnel, the cattle were stabled. What weird noises they made in the night; dogs, sheep, goats, cows and zhos! They all blended in with the scurrying of the rats. Many of the Baltis, during the long cold winter, more or less hibernate in these places. In the open square of our floor was a hole down which the Taki family emptied their garbage to the animals below. I celebrated our arrival by falling halfway through it on the first night of our stay.

There were no glass windows, but merely openings in the walls, which sometimes were filled with wooden lattice work. We had brought glass with us, and by sawing up the boxes which had contained our kit, we made window frames and put glass in them. People came and wonderingly drew their fingers down the panes, never having seen glass before. Pressing their olive-brown faces, encircled by their bobbed raven locks, against the panes they peered at us inside, not realizing that we could see them far better than they could see us. When dust was on the panes, and they could get a reflection of their faces, laughing Balti girls re-arranged, as if in a mirror, their matted hair, or long pigtails, until having watched them kindly, we mischievously pressed our strange white faces on the inside of the glass! What a laughing and hurried scamper there was! They prized even a burnished tin-lid to try to see their playful selves reflected.

We had a kitchen, with a sink in it which we made from stout pieces of wood nailed firmly together, and lined with the tin of our empty paraffin-oil containers. The waste water from it ran out into a hollowed-out, long and slim willow tree-trunk, which was led through the wall at the back of the house, and watered a vine which we sought to cultivate, though without much success.

On the middle floor, where we had our own room, we had a dispensary, and there at set times of the day, we attended the sick. But the patients had special times of their own for attendance; their clock is the sun and quite often their times and ours did not coincide. Nevertheless, we had interesting sessions with them, telling them of the greatest Healer of all, One able to heal spirit, soul and body. We never missed speaking about the Saviour at any dispensary period. At the same time one of us would be out with a medical-box and the Word of God in the homes of those who could not come to the 'sman-nang' or 'medicine-house'. There were many tragic cases of naus-eating, of festering wounds and diseases we had never before encountered, and bones injured by dreadful falls. Those affected by loss of blood their folk could not cope with at all, except to lay them in beds of fine sand, and let the blood drain off into the sand. Often we knelt beside the dying, telling them of the Lord Jesus, the Resurrec-tion and the Life. Many a difficult task we had trying to save life and limb, and became such trusted 'doctors' among these humble mountain people that they even brought cattle to us for advice and treatment. We did our best, which at times did not seem to us to be very much. But supported by the love of God in our hearts, we found that our knowledge of First Aid, our attendance at lectures on Tropical Diseases in King's College, London, our brief training in Dentistry, our presence at operations in the theatre of a Mission Hospital, and our learning to administer an anaesthetic, were all valuable.

Our photographic work was also done in the dispensary. Having taken the pictures we developed the film and made our prints. Rex was the expert in this. The Baltis knew we were at photographic work when they saw a heavy blanket hanging on, and over, the outside of the door to keep out every vestige of light. To have sent our films away for developing would have meant months of waiting, for we were shut in by snow and ice for most of the year, and anything of a parcel-post nature was held back in Kashmir until the passes were said to be open. Mail-runners endeavoured to get through by the lower pass between Kashmir and Baltistan, the Zoji La (11,200 feet) whenever the weather seemed suitable, even in the depths of winter, but they carried letters only. This was done in relay fashion, each man having his own stretch of country to traverse, carrying his short spear-stick for protection, with bells on the end of it to attract attention if he found himself in difficulties. A letter (shoq-shoq) from Britain usually took three months to get to us from its date of posting.[1] Often we would express viewpoints to each other about something we were reading in a newspaper newly come, and then laugh heartily as we realised that the paper had been published at home weeks and weeks earlier. A number of letters arrived at the Dead Letter Office in India before they reached us, and on

1. The word for book in Balti is interesting, 'Shoqbu', which seems to mean 'Son of paper.'

some of the envelopes was written that such a country as Baltistan was unknown. An Indian once said to me before we came into the country that there certainly was a Baluchistan but never a Baltistan!

Except for certain times of the winter when we were enveloped in clouds, photography was possible. In the clear, dry, warm air of a Thibetan summer, in the sparkling frosts of autumn, or in the silver sunshine of Karakoram moonlight when the sky appeared from mountain peak to mountain peak, like a vast and purple regal cushion with the stars shining and tinkling in it like diamonds, we would set up our cameras and take time exposure pictures.

5: In the floods of great waters

In Balti there is no translation of the Psalms, but if ever the words of Psalm 32 : 6 are translated into that language, 'Surely in the floods of great waters they shall not come nigh unto him,' there will be no problem in expressing the phenomenon of which this verse speaks.

In Balti, a 'chhu smen' means a great flood of water, like those experienced in the Karakoram, with the total devastation it brings with it. The Shyock River is one of the main tributaries of the Indus, and has its own incoming rushing torrents one of which is the Hushe Loomba which begins from below Mt. Masherbrum (25,678 feet), with the long Baltoro Glacier, and Mt. Godwin Austen, just beyond. In this area of immensity, beyond man's imagining, a lake forms, fearsomely deep, enclosed by gigantic walls of pillared icy mountains, the only outlet completely blocked by a tower-barrier of ice stretching across the chasm. This holds firm until the titanic pressure of the water within breaks it, and with booms of frightening thunder the deluge plunges, bringing destruction and death for hundreds of miles on its way to the sea. *The Times of India* usually recorded a thousand miles of its devastation.

On one occasion when darkness had fallen, and the moon had not yet appeared, our little door was suddenly pulled open and Iman Admi looked in. 'Come and hear this strange noise,' he said. 'All the people are afraid, and are shouting.' We arose, followed him to an open part of the house, and listened. True enough, close to the base of the mountains, on the other side of our wide valley where the Shyock swept around deep and swift, there was a continual loud rumbling sound. Getting our coats, we hurried towards the river. By this time the moon was rising, and we had not gone far, when we saw water glittering among the apricot trees. The valley was filling with it from mountain to mountain, and people were running in consternation from their homes. We hurried back to ours for a short time of prayer. Iman and Jawani went out into the night to help wherever they could, and we followed with a medicine-box, socks, matches and Bible, resolved to work in the houses nearest the incoming deluge. Men and women, old and young, were hurrying everywhere, carrying vegetables, fruit, hens and skins full of barley flour. An old man, a mullah, was running, as if demented, in advance of the flood, waving a lighted brand and shouting loudly. Off came our coats. Lantern in hand we entered the houses. The people worked desperately, and, by the light of the lanterns, we worked with them. What loads the terror-stricken folk lifted! One young lad lifted a load I could hardly move, and carried it away on his back. The water lapped only six feet from one home we were in. In another my colleague used his headgear to bale out flour into an old blanket, and turned prematurely white-haired when he put it on again!

A young woman was an inspiration. She was so quiet, calm, and ready to help in any way, even to cutting off part of the black string worn by Balti women in the long black plaits of hair which they greatly prized. This was used to tie up the mouth of a bag. Thinking that in a very little time the waters might overflow the houses, we moved swiftly. Our heads banged against the passage supports and the rooftrees of the long low archways of Balti homes, all built like rabbit warrens. The mullah still ran around shouting to the people and calling upon Allah to help. The people were terror-stricken, and we were too, seeing them in such desperate plight. No children were to be seen. Women who at ordinary times would have run away at our approach had lost all shyness, and pulled at us, pleading for us to come and help them. We entered a small flour mill complete with its grind-stones, and gave the women we found there light from our lanterns to enable them to lift the flour from their catch-basket into an old blanket. Time and again we urged the people to move up as high as possible. The moon, fully up now, shone upon a most dismal scene, and we went back to our own house, relieved to find it high and dry. From there we went to find the water level nearest to us, at one of the small barley-flour mills. Iman and a few Baltis were there, and it was evident by the tide mark that the water was receding. A great sea filled the valley, but it was no longer coming up in waves. Our hearts filled with joy and gladness, but we were also deeply saddened as we thought about what was happening in valley after valley as the Shyock joined the Indus and both sped on their course of destruction and death. We returned home, had something to eat, and held a meeting of praise and prayer. Rex sang spiritual songs and I played the accordion. Baltis who were able to come sat around to listen. Two years later, the ice-dam cracked again and burst asunder, and this time our whole valley of villages was engulfed. The house we had known as home was swept away and George Sach, the missionary who was there, escaped with his life by crossing the Thalle La at around 13,000 feet to Ralph Moan at Shigar. Friends and their homes disappeared in the floods. Doghoni, and its surrounding villages, was one of the few Balti areas where the Gospel had ever been preached.

6: *Phru Chik reads his text*

In our roomy house we held the school, entirely of boys, since we were in an Islamic country. Scholars came from five years of age and upwards, including one youth who had a moustache! We began the school with the idea of giving these under-privileged Balti boys the rudiments of an elementary education, but mainly with the hope that in due time they would be able to read the Christian Scriptures for themselves and savingly learn about the Lord Jesus Christ. We brought books, in Urdu, across the passes sufficient for a primary education in reading, writing, arithmetic, geography, and history, for a reasonable number. At that time there were no Christian Scriptures in Balti. This was remedied, to some extent, by the magnificent work of Mr Alfred Read of the Central Asian Mission, the only one in these regions, who could truly be termed a gifted and dedicated linguist. Along with parts of Scripture, he compiled a Grammar and Vocabulary of Balti Thibetan. A difficulty we all encountered was that the Baltis are Shiah Moslems, like the Persians, (Iran); but they speak the farthest western dialect of the Thibetan tongue. This means that their words are best sounded by the vowels, with the consonants of the Thibetan alphabet. But they will have none of this, saying that such lettering is idolatry. Naturally, being Moslems, they like the Arabic forms of writing. To get Thibetan sounds expressed, as they should be, by Persic-Arabic lettering, is no easy task, and a literate Balti looking at it is inclined to shake his head, and to say that the letters do not represent at all the sounds of the Balti-Thibetan tongue. For all literary work we found it best to keep to Urdu.

We missionaries took the Scripture lessons only. At first, it was necessary for three of us to speak before the boys could understand what we were saying. One of us said a little in English, Iman put it into Urdu, Piyara Dost into Thibetan Balti. Most of the class soon learned to read Urdu, and could stand up and read it aloud, and write it. And we too made progress with it. We lacked exercise books for written work, but the scholars had broad flat pieces of wood on which they coated a white soluble substance dug out from a mountain, which when dry, left a smooth surface on which the boys wrote with pen-like bits of wood dipped into a darkish watery clay. One could not but admire their penmanship which often looked like a work of art. Writing from right to left, and beginning at what we would consider the end of a book, we too got down to reading, writing, and speaking Urdu.

In our readings of the Scriptures in the class-room, now and again we had strikes and rebellions! These usually happened when a reader came to the words, 'Jesus Christ, the Son of God'. He would stop just there, and no-one could move him to read them. On being questioned why he would not read the words, he might reply, 'Well, you see, this is not our religion.' Our usual answer to this was, that at one time it was not our religion either, but that the Eternal God had shown us that this was part of his revelation for our salvation, and that he should read the words. The boy would merely shake his head, expressing a decided, 'No.' The next boy was asked to stand up and read the inspired words and the whole verse with them. But he, too, would read only till he came to the words, 'Jesus Christ, the Son of God,' and there he stopped. Questioned, he might say that his folks had told him that he was not to read such words. 'Very well, the next boy stand up, and read the verse.' He responded in the same way, as they all did. A silent and sullen class of boys sat facing us. We could not and would not compel any boy to read this great truth about the Lord Jesus, but we had to keep it clear before them that this was the Christian faith.

At the close of school lessons the boys came to us in a group saying that they did not believe the Christian Gospel, and would no longer attend a school where it was taught; and they handed in their books. We told them that we were the servants of Christ and must teach His Gospel, that the school was His, and that we must be faithful to the charge which He had given to us. If they did not want the school, we told them, they need not attend it, and we would use some of our school time to come to their villages to tell them about the Lord Jesus. Away they went with many a 'salaam' and our hearts with them. Next day we were out and about, and in a 'grong' (village) some of these little rebels would come up to us, their eyes all a twinkle, their sheepskin skullcaps askew, and while listening, would lean upon their polo-sticks like seasoned veterans of their national game. Polo means ball, and every boy as a toddler begins to learn it by hitting stones with his little 'po-lo' stick. There they would stand, in their long gown-smocks, for all the world like a band of Wee Willie Winkies! They laughed, so did I. Who would not laugh with the merry laugh of a child! 'Aha', I would say, 'Here I am then. I told you I would come. Now, please, kindly listen to what I have to say to you about the Lord Jesus Christ.'

Next day one or two might turn up at the school, and a few more the following day, and so on. Away, full swing again, went the school. And then again rebellion! In the deep cleft vales of the Karakoram, even in a humble Mission-School, we heard the echo of a cry long ago, 'We have a law, and by our law He ought to die, because He made Himself the Son of God.' Mullahs spoke severely against us. It was said that some had threatened to pull down the building. This we did not believe, for there are no kinder folk than the Baltis. So it went on, this battle between friends.

Phru Chik the brightest of our scholars, was a poor boy who was always in rags. He was an able reader of Urdu, but had rebelled with the rest when asked to read words which stated directly, or implied that the Lord Jesus Christ was the Son of God. One day in the Scripture lesson this young lad stood up to read his verse, and the offending words were in it. He read them. Every boy in the class gazed at him. There was an intense silence. Questions were written on every face. What had happened? Had he lost his senses? What would be the outcome of this? How could he be so foolish, and so unfaithful to Islam, and to us all? He looked around them all, every eye in the class intent upon him, and ours also. 'You need not be surprised', he said, 'I can read these words now. I have Jesus Christ in my heart.' From that moment he boldly took his stand for Christ. We rejoiced with trembling. We had seen what can be, comparatively speaking, a rare event among Islamic peoples, the conversion of a soul to Christ. Resonsibility was laid upon us to give the young lad all the friendship and fellowship possible. He took to his humble home a copy of the Scriptures in Urdu, and developed spiritually; but soon social pressures were exerted upon him and his people, who were in no position to defend him. To public knowledge he had now become apostate, and was a 'kafir' in the eyes of all. However kindly the Baltis are by nature some of them are very hard of heart because of their religion. In a short time we had to give Phru Chik a home with ourselves, with Iman, Jawani and Piyara, all converts themselves from Islam. He was to know later what angry blows were, but he stood the test. That old home of ours was taken away in the great flood of glacial waters, but there are memories that remain associated with it, memories of things of eternal value.

7: *Karakoram man of the book*

A day's walking east from Doghoni is Khapalu, and soon after our arrival in Doghoni, Iman Admi went there for a few necessities. On returning he told us that he had met

[25]

a Christian in the town and that he was coming along to see us. We could hardly believe it. A Christian there! It was the end of the unevangelised world to us.

Some time later the Christian came along. He was a young man, evidently well educated, and of North India extraction, speaking Balti, Urdu and English! We were greatly drawn to him. He was distressed, and very soon he told us that he was having a testing time because he was a Christian. A copy of the New Testament in Urdu had come into his possession, and through reading it he had become a believer in the Lord Jesus Christ. As he was reputed to be a Seiyid, a nominal descendant of Muhammad, many Baltis paid him polite respect as they passed him on the village paths. He had stopped going to the mosque to worship, and had been praying that Christians would come to Baltistan. With obvious joy he told us, 'You are an answer to my prayers. God has sent you here for fellowship with me. My father is very angry with me, and life at home has become trying.'

Back he went to Khapalu to suffer the antagonism of his family, and the community. He was eventually ordered out of his home. Having kept in touch with him we asked him to come and join us, which he did, teaching us both Urdu and Balti. Piyara Dost was the Lord's provision for us at such a time, and it did us good spiritually to have him with us. He was truly a godly man, and a great asset to Iman Admi as a fellow teacher in the school where the boys respected him.

In due time he and I went to Shigar, our other mission centre, where he took charge of our school, four days' journey from Doghoni, to which he returned after a month or two. I often hoped for his return and one sunny afternoon he arrived, Phru Chik with him. I went joyfully out to meet them, but I had never seen them look so downcast before. There was such a strangeness about their droll silence that I began to laugh. They quietly told me that I would not laugh if I had suffered as they had, and they related their story.

In a certain village an angry man had accosted them and asked if they were two of the Christians from Doghoni. They admitted they were; whereupon he severely thrashed both of them. They had reached me with aching limbs and bones. Jawani was there with me, and we saw to their comfort. I was very displeased, and told them I would look for this man, and talk to him. They advised me to do no such thing. But I was determined, and the day came when I was in his village. I went around it, calling at every house, mentioning him by name, but no one would admit to knowing him, or that such a man lived in their 'grong.'

I wrote to my colleague about the 'jati mi', or 'fearsome man', asking Rex to look out for him, and possibly have a word with him; but one day I received a letter from him telling me not to look for the man any more. He had seen him when he, himself, was sitting among Baltis as one of them. (We dressed like the people, were bearded, and often were thought to be Baltis. They would give us the usual Balti greetings as we passed by. Sometimes when we turned around afterwards we might find that they also had turned around, rather puzzled). Rex had heard the man's name mentioned, and out of the corner of his eye had seen him. He said in his letter to me, 'Give up looking for him. I have seen him, and that is enough. He is a wild bad man.' In the Lord's mercy we had no more trouble from him.

Piyara became an eager student of the Scriptures, and an apt preacher of the Gospel. His enthusiasm was refreshing, and he did what he could to make others interested. His step-brother died and he told us that he would like to return to Khapalu to the home from which he had been cast out. I too had to leave Shigar, but in another direction. Three months passed before I returned again to be with him in Shigar. Tired and hungry I arrived there after many a mile over desert sands, mountains, snows and rivers, and for most of that time had not slept in a bed. For most of the summer months one can sleep on the ground in these Thibetan uplands and we were adept in our choice of places of rest for the night. Piyara Dost was kindness itself to me on my arrival at Shigar Mission House.

We had not been long in each other's company when he said that he had something important to tell me. It was that he was married! 'Married!' I exclaimed. 'Who married you? A mullah?' And surprise of surprises! 'No', he said. 'We married ourselves.' I was amazed. 'Married yourselves! How did you do that?' And Piyara told me how it happened. An old man who was dying had sent for him saying that he wanted to speak to him. He went, and was received with kindness and respect. The sick man said to him, 'I am glad you have come. I am dying, and I am leaving my only child in this world, a daughter. I have kept her beside me, but soon I must leave her. She is now a young woman, and I would like to see her settled before I go. Will you marry her? I have some land. It will be yours if you do.' I sat silent. Piyara continued, 'I told him that I would have to think prayerfully about such a proposal, and would have to see and talk things over with his daughter as to whether we were suitable for each other and could make a match of it.' Calling the old dying Balti his father, he continued, 'My father then said that he had a Book wrapped up in cloth to preserve it, for it was a Holy Book, and he would not let it touch the ground. But he was sorry he could not read it; and it was not a Moslem book.. Maybe I could read it to him.' Piyara unwrapped the book and found that it was an Urdu New Testament, and, he said, 'Day by day I read it to my father. He became a believer in the Lord Jesus Christ, and died trusting in Him.' Piyara continued, 'Before he died his daughter and I met and spoke together, and we found that we liked each other. I asked her to be my wife. She agreed, and my father was very happy indeed.'

I listened quietly while Piyara Dost went on with his unique story, saying that he had had to act quickly lest his fiancée, who was still a Moslem, might be taken and married to one of that faith. He did not know where my colleague and I were, the only missionaries in these regions. As far as we knew, he was the only Christian in the land of Baltistan at that time. Iman Jawani and Phru Chik were in Kashmir. He felt that he did not want a mullah to have anything to do with his marriage, but that he could see to it himself in a Christian way. So I listened to the story of the first Christian marriage in Baltistan. It is the only one of which I have knowledge. I have never heard of another. Piyara stood beside me where I sat, and speaking softly said, 'I said to my fiancée that she, being still a Moslem, and a Balti, should bring two witnesses according to the custom of the land. I would bring my two witnesses, but it was to be a Christian wedding, and it was to take place in the Mission House. She came with her two witnesses, and I had mine. They could not see mine, and asked where they were. I told them they were with me, my Lord and Saviour, and my Bible, and I held forth the Book. While they sat, I stood and prayed, saying to the Lord that He knew that I loved the woman, and that she loved me, and that before Him we wished to take each other as man and wife. And so we were married.'

I sat with bowed head knowing that I had listened to something which had never happened before in these parts. He stood silent beside me. It was a sacred moment, and I knew that whatever I said must have wisdom from the Lord in it. He spoke first. It helped me. He said, 'Well, if you are not happy about what has been done we are quite willing to travel to Kashmir and be married all over again in a Christian meeting-place in Srinagar.' A fortnight's journey across the roof of the world! I quickly thought things through. 'No,' I said, 'you and your wife are married in the sight of the Lord. Everything is in order. We shall have prayer together and I shall commend you both to the Lord.' This we did with solemnised but happy hearts. She became a follower of the Lord.

Through thick and thin Piyara Dost stood with us. As day followed day I admired him more. It was rather a sad occasion when we had to part, he to remain at his post, and I to go to the Afghan Frontier. After prayer we exchanged turban cloths, and said goodbye. But what a delightful surprise it was, one morning much later, when there was a knock at my door, and when I called to the person knocking to come in, the door opened and there was Piyara! Hundreds of miles he had travelled to see me. I asked him many things during our conversation, including the all-important questions, 'What of the Lord? Are you still following Him?' He looked at me, and the well-known smile came on his face. 'Till death,' he said. 'See, once I lost all for Him. I had nothing. Now the Lord has given me wife, child and lands.'

His last letter to me was in English, and some of it can be shared. 'Dear In Him, Hoping allways and remembering you in our everyday's prayers and trusting same from

you. I am sorry to say that I could not write you so long.
May God, Father and Lord bless you for His own sake.
Amen. It is so long since I did not heard any from you.
The time of the 2nd Coming of our Lord the Christ is just
near then wee will see our dear Master & Shepherd by
our week eyes. Halleujah! Philippians, 1.3–11. Best wishes
from us all and from Schoolboys. Yours in Lord.' Then
comes his well-known signature. His 'week eyes' have
since seen his 'dear Master & Shepherd,' and all that was
mortal of him is laid away in his Karakoram earthly
home till the great day when we shall meet again. He was
one of the most sincere Christians I ever knew.

8: *Butsa Karim*

From the neighbouring village of Blaghar, a man came
for me, requesting me to return with him to see his
younger brother who was ill. We set off together and soon
were among the small fields rescued from almost naked
rock. With no rainfall nothing grows on them without
the ingenious Balti system of irrigation, where the ter-
raced cascades utilise every drop of water possible. Precious water is diverted from streams flowing from the
snows and glaciers. It is hard to believe it, but it is so;
there are what might be called diminutive artificial
glaciers made by the Baltis, where water is actually stored
in animal skin bags, between alternate layers of straw,
earth and pebbles, the water freezing into solid ice during
the winter, and melting the following spring for agricul-
tural and domestic purposes. Deficient in iodine and sea

salts, it is not as good as drinking water, and this is probably one of the reasons why there is so much serious goitre in the land.

After many a scramble over rock and through water we reached the home. As usual, wood-smoke filled the place; I could not stand upright but had to move about on my knees. My eyes smarted, and I could not see. I had to come out again. They brought out the sick lad, Butsa Karim (Boy Karim), and laid him on the ground in front of me. One of his legs appeared to be seriously poisoned and in a very diseased condition. Various Balti medical men and their remedies had been tried, but to no avail. The last hope was the missionary, and he was not a doctor. It is a strange thing to live among a people for whom there is no skilled medical or surgical help whatsoever.

My chloroform was finished but I did what I could, as quickly as I could, with the scalpel, and after that there were weeks of washing and dressing as I tried to help him. Lice crawled over my hands as I worked. He had some terrible sores. They would have been termed bed-sores, but there was no bed. He lay on hard, matted and filthy rags. Had he been bleeding much he would have been laid in a layer of fine sand. Two or three hours daily I spent with him, ever washing and dressing his sores. The vermin were horrible, hideous. I used to hurry home in utter torment. One day a word of Scripture came to me as I ran. It reached me in a way different from the usual interpretations of it! It was a word of the Psalmist, 'The ploughers ploughed upon my back, they made long their furrows.'

It was disheartening work. Healing seemed hopeless. Day after day I spoke to Butsa of the Saviour, praying that the Holy Spirit would bring him to faith. When I did so, silent crouching figures in the smoky darkness came to life, and finding voice, interrupted me, and argued, as I read and quoted words of eternal life to the sick boy. 'How could God have a Son? Had He a wife?' they asked. They were scornful and impertinent. They despised Christ, and like many other Moslems, spat on the ground at the mention of His Name. Often I had a very heavy heart for the lad, and especially when it became quite apparent that he would soon die in a land where there was neither doctor nor nurse, schoolmaster nor evangelist, but merely two missionaries, weak mixtures of them all.

Shortly afterwards, Rex arrived, having traversed the rocky paths from Shigar. He had been fascinated, *en route*, by seeing snow leopards. Like myself, he was rather a scarecrow-looking Balti, and just as verminous. We could put our hands down the neck of our 'gonmo' (smock) and draw out lice in the palms of our hands. We could not but laugh when we looked at each other. We could have protected and preserved ourselves by living after the style of 'pakha sahibs', but we chose the other way and lived, as much as was possible, like the people around us. I took my colleague to see Butsa Karim before I left for Shigar, and in much sorrow spoke to the lad of the love of God in Christ Jesus, and whispered sweet and precious verses of the Word of God to him. He languidly smiled up at me as I urged him to commit himself to the Lord Jesus. 'I am going away far from you, Butsa Karim; trust in Jesus; we shall not meet here again; trust in Jesus who died for sinners, then we shall meet in heaven.' Sullen faces around us were dark and forbidding as we parted with prayer in that poor hovel of a home, I soon to pass close by on the way to Shigar, and he soon to pass into eternity. Generally speaking the Baltis are a likeable and kindly people, but Islam has marred many of them, giving them traits that are far from pleasant.

Many a short day and long dark night passed, and many another Butsa Karim I saw among the great mountains before I returned to the deep valley where stood the village of Blaghar, to stand by the mound of earth which marked Karim's grave. There was another mound close by, that of an old man who was much afraid to die. I remembered his cries. I knew him well. He had befriended us during opposition, and I had often been with him during part of his agonising last days. It is not playing with words to say that there are peoples in the Himalaya and the Karakoram who are hopeless in their helplessness, and helpless in their hopelessness, and, because of the political situations, we never hear of them at all.

9: Tshuntse Ali

Around our home in Doghoni were the graves of the village, the house of one of the leading families, and the 'masjid' or mosque. If a funeral took place we could hear and see the expressions of hopeless sorrow; we were called into the big man's house in sickness; and we were acquainted with the comings and goings at the mosque, and the councils held outside the main door. One day there was a heated argument, the central figures being a poor woman, seemingly a widow, her ragged little boy, and an angry looking man. We watched from the flat roof of our home, and heard the widow passionately plead her cause before the council of men seated on the ground. We pitied her and her boy, but, of course, could not interfere. Besides, we had difficulty in understanding what it was all about. When the council dispersed, the angry man went away with a smile on his face.

We enquired into the case, and were told that the late husband of the woman had worked for a man from whom he held a field which had helped him to support his wife and boy, and for a time after the death of her husband the field was used by the poor widow, but now at the time of seed sowing, the owner wanted it back again. Fields are very valuable in Baltistan. Many a time I saw Baltis making fields on bare rock! With huge baskets upon their backs they would bring heavy loads of silt, from dried-up river beds, and spread them upon the most unproductive looking ground it was possible to see.

A few days later the council of men sat to discuss the widow's case once more. Various arguments and opinions were expressed, but the judgment given was that the man be given back his field. A moment's consideration and pity from him would have let the widow keep it. We prayed for her and her child and asked the Lord to enable us to be of help to them in their difficulty. We were glad when the boy Tshuntse Ali (Little Ali) came to our door with five eggs to sell, and we gave him the price of a dozen. He was a bundle of lousy rags, and we asked him to come in and wait a little, while we considered what we could do for him in the way of clothes. Getting his shirt off we saw it was one that Jawani had given him, one that had been mine before it was Jawani's! Our discarded shirts and other garments were quite popular, and they passed from one to another down the social scale until only the neckband and a few shreds of them were left! Rex got out one of his best khaki ones and made ready to wash the young mountaineer, though all of us would fain have had a hand in this.

It was Tshuntse Ali's first real wash for many a day.

Soap and water were soon applied. I was getting ready to go out into the villages with my medical box. Piyara was to go with me, but he persisted in helping with the bath until Rex chased him away. Before we went we saw the Balti laddie looking so fresh and happy with a nice, long, clean shirt on him, in the way Baltis like to wear shirts, smocklike, before we set off. He was asked if he would like to attend school, and he came that very day! We had got a new scholar, and acquiring some Yarkandi cloth we soon had Hassein, the 'hilam' (tailor), busy making a warm smock for Tshuntse Ali, who used to come in to family worship at times. Here he heard the Word of life as well as in the school. We kept in mind and practice the word of the Master about suffering little children to come to Him.

10: *A woman of Muntaru*

We did not come to know her name, which is strange, for she was a pleasant and motherly person, and the 'zanzos', or wife, of humble Wali, whom we liked very much. They lived in Muntaru, a village not far from Doghoni, and we had to think of her as a 'Muntarupang-o', or 'a woman from Muntaru.' We made the acquaintance of them both when Wali came to us for medical help for her. Piyara and I went with him. He was rather deaf, which was a disadvantage when we talked with him about his sick wife. Arriving at their home in Muntaru we met Mrs Wali who could not walk because of a leg very badly poisoned from the knee downwards. Pus was running out near the ankle.

When I told Piyara that a cutting would have to be made, he would not stay, but would return when it was over. Long before, a splinter of wood had run into the foot, and the result was this painful and inconvenient condition of the leg. Zanzos Wali had also a large goitre, but she was kindly and cheery, exchanging greetings with us as she lay on the hardened mud verandah of their lowly home. I had to open up the foot. She bore this bravely. The suction of the pus could be felt in her limb. Pressure below the knee down the calf of the leg brought it running out thickly from the cutting in the foot. It meant weeks of daily attention, and I used up every handkerchief I possessed in hot fomentations. What a joyful day it was for us all when she was on her feet again and able to walk about!

As in many another home the entering of Wali's was a welcome opportunity of doing good and of bringing the Good News of a Saviour. Many a reading of Holy Scripture we had, and many a prayer we offered, in that primitive Karakoram home. It was a joy to be there. Wali himself was so friendly, and she so patient and kind. Others coming in sat around and heard about the Lord, and naturally enough there was also homely conversation on various subjects including illness. Cures were suggested for different troubles. Wali held the floor one morning as he talked about his headaches. One of the suggestions for a remedy was put forward by a burly, dull-looking chap. I could not follow what it was; it sounded rather strange. 'Me go i'kha,' or 'fire on the head,' was his description of it. Wali looked rather apprehensive. A piece of metal was to be heated in a fire until it was red-hot and then applied to the aching head of the sufferer! I had to say with much firmness, that such a proposed act to help headaches was nonsense, and that whoever did such a thing was very foolish. Wali, despite his deafness, got the gist of it all and was relieved by my words.

One morning Rex returned, happy and excited, from his medical rounds, and asked me if I had noticed anything unusual in the Wali home where I had been the night before. 'No,' I replied. 'Well, man,' he said, 'when I was there this morning I heard a baby sound below the rags that cover Zanzos Wali, and I asked the meaning of it. They turned back the ragged coverings and showed me a brown baby girl who had been born to them during the night. I too became excited! This was their ninth child. Seven of them had died. The infant mortality rate of Lesser Thibet is shocking beyond words. Their little boy now had a sister. Would she live? The harshness of primitive conditions in the birth of a child and its upbringing there is beyond the telling. Being kept warm during the winter in a sheepskin bag lined with dung is not the worst of them. They named the little one Miriam, after the sister of Moses, and by a mistake in the teachings of Muhammad, after Mary, the mother of Jesus. It was a token of respect for us also. Rex really took her to his heart, but the thought, distressingly, was ever with us that Miriam would not live long. We wondered how she could. We were determined to do everything possible for her and her parents. My colleague decided to do some tailoring, and managed to make something of a smock, or 'gonmo' for the little brown thing. It was of rough Balti home-spun, and he took it with fond delight to the happy parents. Zanzos Wali used to send Wali along to us asking for advice whenever she thought there was anything wrong with her baby girl. Sometimes Miriam was rather a puzzle for us two lone bachelors. Sometimes there were knit brows for Nono Miriam.

Time passed, and the Walis seemed to be getting along

satisfactorily. I had the usual journeys over sands, mountains and rivers, between our mission posts. I said farewell to them and other families, and it was months before I saw them again. On returning to Doghoni, Rex gave me the sad news that Miriam had died, and that I must go to see her parents who were much distressed and discouraged. On seeing me coming the mother rose from the midst of a group of women, and running to me threw herself at my feet, hitting her forehead on my sandals, and weeping bitterly. Her cries for Nono Miriam were heart-rending to hear. Returning home with her I sought to comfort her, speaking to her about the 'Man of sorrows who was acquainted with grief.'

On a beautiful morning she came along to us bringing some fruit from her meagre store. Humbly she offered it to us and we gladly accepted it. We were having Bible reading and prayer and we invited her to stay. Sitting in a corner near the door, she listened intently, and went away at the close of worship with words of thanks. We thought that a work of the Holy Spirit had been done in her heart, giving her assurance of salvation.

Shortly afterwards we saw her again. A festival was on, and the Baltis were entranced with their sports and sword-dancing. We were happy mingling among them. Boys gathered around us, many of them our schoolboys, a merry laughing crowd. We shook with laughter as Zanzos Wali, seeing them in our way, dashed among them, playfully striking out at them and sending the happy vagabonds running hither and thither. She was an encouraging blink of sunshine for us in our trying Islamic world.

[39]

11: *Kang Po-Lo*

We introduced soccer, or 'kang po-lo', into Baltistan. It had never been played there before. We did not mean to do so. It came about because of our school games. Doghoni, unlike Blaghar, had no polo ground. We went to the latter place to play, and thrilled its villagers to the core. Their land is the home of polo, and any village of any consequence has its own polo ground, unless it is too close to the mountain bases, as was Doghoni. What players the Baltis are! Horsemanship par excellence! They ride bareback, without stirrups, and sometimes without reins, bending low to hit the po-lo, or ball, with their home-made sticks. I never got the length of playing polo among the Baltis, but, of course, there were players' injuries to patch up at times. Our home was the nearest house to the ground at Shigar, and abutted on that part from which most of the po-lo musicians came. It was referred to as the 'mong-grong', or the 'village of music.' We were well acquainted with the game, the players, and their band.

Soccer matches in Blaghar were our 'pièce-de-résistance', and were arranged for our schoolboys' sakes, to encourage them to keep coming to school, and to encourage others to come and so learn to read the Holy Scriptures, and hear the Gospel. After each game we spoke to the crowds gathered around us about the Saviour, and sang our songs of praise to the accompaniment of our accordion.

Crowds of spectators came, and crowds of players. And those who were onlookers, for a time, eventually dashed on to the 'jing', and became players too. Every child, it seemed, who could walk, and every male person to the very oldest, who could make his way on to the polo ground felt it was his right to play. Only cripples, and those who did not feel very well, sat around to watch the game. We marshalled the sides, and the serried ranks of them, like miniature armies, stood facing each other. Elementary rules of the game were explained to them with many an enthusiastic response of 'Ya! Ya!' ('Yes! Yes!'). And did they understand the rules? Of course they did! 'Ong-a! Ong-a!' ('Certainly! Certainly!'). But how these laws of the game were to be applied was beyond our understanding. My fellow-missionary captained one side, and I the other. One of us blew a whistle; the other kicked the ball; the game was on! What a merry riot! Men and boys were bowled over like ninepins. Rex disappeared one moment, and I the next. Rugby scrums formed all over the place. Somewhere in the middle of the largest scrum, like a monster human beehive, of kicking legs and wrestling arms, of sheepskins, goatskins and fluttering rags, was the ball. The fun of it was overpowering, as others, recovering their breath, hurled themselves time and again into the writhing mass. We laughed till the tears ran down our cheeks, indeed, until we were sore, and had to lie down for relief on the 'po-lo-jing.' An amazing moment arrived when the great scrum began to move and heave, bodies fell to the sides of it, and someone dishevelled, but still fighting, would emerge with the ball, dash away across the polo ground, through the fields and on to the mountain paths, with scores behind him shouting, 'Laqpong mit! Laqpong mit!' ('No hands! No hands!'). We watched them strung out against the barren mountain background till they disappeared from view. We had to sit down with the others, and await their return. The game began again with those who were able to play. How they roared with laughter when my colleague or I bit the dust! Even loud applause! After the game we donned our sheepskin coats, gathered as many around us as would listen, spoke to them of the love and salvation of God revealed in Christ Jesus, and accompanied by the accordion sang Gospel songs to them, including, 'Mihrban! Mihrban! Mihrban!' a beautiful song of the loving-kindness and mercy of God, in the Lord Jesus Christ. They had never seen a football before. That was not of great importance. Our Balti friends would profit little by our bringing one. But that those who had not heard the Gospel were now hearing it, as important beyond the telling. It was part of the answer to the apostolic question, 'How shall they hear without a preacher?' We knew that we were sent to preach Christ and Him crucified, in Lesser Thibet, and we did so. The same feet with which we ran about in 'kang po-lo,' had traversed hazardous ways in a land, parts of which are unexplored and unclimbed, and written about by Eric Shipton in his book, 'Blank On The Map.' In a measure the Scripture had an aptness for us, 'How beautiful upon the mountains are the feet of him that bringeth good tidings of good, that publisheth salvation.'

After such a time in Blaghar my colleague became ill with what appeared to be typhoid fever, a death-dealing disease of Central Asia. I judged it to be typhoid by his weakness, severe headaches, high temperature and delirium. There was no one who could advise otherwise. Prayerfully I did what I could for him, and was glad and thankful to the Lord when he bettered. We had to be watchful in our drinking of water, which was from streams, rivers and from melted snow. If from a stream we scanned to the farthest bounds, and if there was a human habitation in sight we refrained from drinking from it, no matter how severe our thirst.

12: *Friends and neighbours*

In both Doghoni and Shigar, our Mission Centres, we had the houses to live in nearest to the village graves. We did not object to that, but we could never become reconciled in heart and mind with the sad funerals where the mourners cried in unrestrained grief, the men weeping and beating upon their breasts, and the women sitting on the flat roof-tops gesticulating their farewells, and screaming pathetically. The graves were dug in the shape of a rectangle. A cavity was cut out in one of the longer sides at the bottom of the grave and the body deposited in it. Stone slabs were then placed to enclose the dead, and the burial place filled up. At such sad times we expressed our sympathy with the bereaved, longing that they might know the Lord Jesus Christ, the Resurrection and the Life.

Sometimes, in the midst of sickness, sorrow and death, there were events in which we became involved, as in the case of Mahmoud and his mother, who, with the rest of their family, lived near to us. One night, in Doghoni, when I was going to rest there was a loud knocking at the door, and on my opening it I was confronted by a group of Baltis, their brands of brushwood burning in the darkness. They were with Mahmoud who asked me to come and help his mother who was weak and ill. Donning a coat over my night-clothes I went with him and the noisy

crowd to his home, where as many as possible crowded
into the room where Api (grandma) was seated. The
brands flickered and flamed, casting strange shadows
about us, and on the greased faces of Mahmoud's friends.
One was apt to smile at their greased faces, but the time
came when I had to laugh at my own. Speaking kindly
and inquiringly to Api I could see that I could not help
her very much. What disappointment all around when I
apologetically said so! 'Nonsense,' said some. 'You must
have something that could help Api among all these
bottles and tins you have in your 'sman' (medicines).
You have helped many; you can help Api; think a bit
more.' I failed to persuade them that I could not help
much, and had to think of something that would be
harmless for Api. Finally, I thought that I might give her
a small dose of castor-oil. Out into the night we all tumbled, for all wanted to accompany me to the dispensary.
There we marched. It was cold. I was glad I had a coat
over my night-clothes; these so-necessary coats, especially
our sheepskin ones! An old man once brought mine from
Doghoni to Shigar. Quite innocently he slept in it every
night, and equally innocently I wore it, giving myself
another horrifying invasion of lice.

Around the dispensary we all crowded and I let them
see me take down the big bottle of castor-oil. I held it aloft
in one hand and a spoon in the other. The return proces-
sion began with them still being held on high. What interest! What relief for many of them to see Api get her
modest dosage of castor-oil! All went off happily to their
homes. A few days later I was speaking to Mahmoud and,
when I enquired about his mother, he said that the medicine I had given her had, he thought, helped her, but that
she was still quite tired and weak. I told him that what I
had given her would not help her much, and that I did

not think she would survive the winter. My surmise proved correct. She died. Her funeral was a sad occasion, and she was buried not many yards from the mission-house.

Mahmoud came saying that prayers would have to be recited by a mullah for a few days, and seeing that the winter was now upon us, would I lend him a tent to shelter the mullah? I gave him one. Great was my surprise, when the tent was erected, to see that it was right over the grave of Api! There the mullah lived, praying and chanting for forty days! On their appeal to me I had let them carry on for that time, and there the man sat under the snow-covered tent. A fire burned in it, and when it was re-turned it was unusable, for it was completely blackened by wood smoke. Nevertheless I felt much for Mahmoud and the many around us in their spiritual darkness. He built a low wall around the grave, and I saw him one morning lean over it, shaking his head in his own sorrow-ful way. My heart went out to him in sympathy.

Then someone else died, and Apo Taki came begging a loan of the tent which we had cleaned. I told him that I could not lend it to him after what had happened the time before. I also told him that according to the Christian faith, the dead should be left in the hands of God and not be prayed for; and it was all-important that we should know the Lord Jesus Christ – Him who was dead and now ever lives. He smiled incredulously at me, shaking his head condescendingly, and saying, 'It is our way at times like these. There is good in it. It is just that you are not one of us, and do not understand us. Please lend us the tent.' Regretfully, I refused to do so. Still smiling at my ignorance of what he thought was the true religion of the Baltis, he went away.

A short time afterwards I was out at the back of the

house and noticed that something was missing from the main outer door. This door was in two halves lengthwise; it let one in and out of a small square and up a wooden stair before entering the house proper. It was opened and shut on a swivel basis by an elongated piece at the end of each half of the door turning round for movement in a hollowed piece of wood set into the ground. I could not take it in that one half of the door was gone! But where was it? I knew the answer. It was being used, of course, to make part of a shack for a mullah over the newly-dug grave! I went around the corner to see. Sure enough, there was Apo Taki, with a few more, busy erecting over the filled-in burial-place, a small hut for Moslem prayer. Half of the door was part of it! I was greeted with smiles, and could not but smile too. 'Ho! Ho!' I said. 'You are a most amazing lot of people right enough! Fancy, coming and taking away part of a man's doors!' Said old Apo Taki, 'Well, you see, you would not give us a loan of the tent!' Then again, our house belonged to him; he was our landlord!

Much time was spent by myself and fellow-workers in learning Balti and Urdu. The former is a dialect of Thibetan, and is, as Alfred Read says, 'a collection of independent short syllables. However many syllables the word may contain, each one must be given equal emphasis and never be cut short.' Both languages have short, medium and long vowels, with consonants, labial, dental, nasal, aspirate, and gutteral. Piyara made us laugh sometimes when he imitated a European speaking partially learned Urdu to a national. It was funny and absurd. We were deeply indebted to him for helping us with both tongues.

In the language lessons minor points of interest appeared such as words that corresponded with each other, for example, 'kaun' and 'koi' in Urdu with 'co' meaning 'who' in Gaelic, and the phrases, 'Koi hai?' in Urdu and 'Co tha sin' in Gaelic meaning, 'Who is there?' or 'Is there anyone there?' There was also the 'kya' in Urdu and the 'cia' in Gaelic meaning 'What?' or 'How?' There were the similarities of the words for dog, Urdu 'kutta,' Gaelic 'cu,' Thibetan 'khi,' pronounced 'kee' as in the Welsh word for dog. A scholar in Celtic would have smiled at our amateurish discoveries. Nevertheless they could set one thinking about the derivation of language.

How important it is that a missionary should know the language of the people amongst whom he works! We failed many a time in this line of communication. It was amusing one day in Northern Kashmir when a high rank-ing British officer said to me that he was waiting for the 'qabr.' We spoke in English and once or twice he used this Urdu word meaning 'grave.' I was puzzled until I realised that he meant to say 'khabar' meaning 'news' or 'message.' It was just that he was not good at using gut-terals. He was waiting for news!

Many a time we felt sorry that we had stomachs, and therefore had to eat. Food was often scarce. We could get a rough barley with which to make a kind of porridge. Milk was of weak quality, usually from goats. The butter made from it being churned in a goatskin was far from clean and palatable. In a sheepskin we kept flour from which we made 'chapati,' (unleavened cakes). Meat was a scarce commodity. For months we never tasted it. Tea we brought into the country. When it was finished we had water. Apricots in their season, fresh, and during the winter, dried, were in constant supply. One day, Jawani brought in to us a black and yellow concoction, which Rex tasted, and reported that obviously the taste of it had to be acquired. But there was nothing else. We had to get it to the back of our throats and swallow it down. It could

[47]

not be anything out of order for Jawani was a Kashmiri. Before our time of reading the Word, praying and singing to the Lord, he came in and we asked him what he had given us. He said that it was 'yujidi.' We had never heard of it before, nor have we heard of it since, and he had difficulty in explaining what it was. It had some connection with the scrapings of the inside of the paunch of a sheep.

What a field we were in for geographers, geologists, botanists, explorers, climbers, naturalists, linguists, and historians! But we had little spare time for anything of that nature; we were there for one purpose only, that of making Christ known to the people, and we lived and worked by all necessary means to that end. There was, later on, geographical recognition for travels and work in the land, but fulfilling the Divine Commission was our supreme purpose.

When travelling by water we used the 'zach,' a craft made from twenty or more inflated animal-skins. To inflate these was a dirty job done by the owners. What a maze of tyings on the legs of the skins to keep them watertight! They were far from being gay balloons, but far more useful, though some of them sprang a leak! Our longest sail in a 'zach' was of about ten miles on the Shyock, from Khapalu to Doghoni. We admired the skill of our Balti steersman. All went well except for my disembarking too soon and finding myself up to the neck in water. It was a bit of a scramble to get back on board. Usually, in our travels we were on the move by daybreak, termed by the Baltis, 'nam langpa' (the rising of the sky). They do not measure time clockwise, but time their day by light upon the mountains, and by the sun when it or its rays can be seen.

13: Return to Srinagar

After our first winter and spring in Doghoni, when we were shut in by snow and ice, summer came, the passes were open, and we divested ourselves of our homespun smocks and trousers, each leg two feet wide, put on shirts, shorts and puttees, clipped off our beards, shaved, and set off on our sixteen days' journey to Srinagar. Iman, Rga and Jawani accompanied us.

Our way out of Baltistan to Kashmir was by the lower of the usable passes, the Zoji La, at 11,580 feet. At Kharmang we saw the spider web rope-bridge, and were glad that we did not have to cross it. It swung its threadlike way across the noisy torrents of the Indus, like a long rope-ladder, which in much smaller size was used by Baltis to climb the face of crags and heights, unscalable by hand and foot alone.

To be shut in by snows is a unique experience. And such an experience during illness can be awkward, especially if one develops something which possibly needs surgery, as when, during my second Karakoram winter, because of an acute pain I thought that I might be developing appendicitis. It was quite a thought to look forward a whole year before we could set out across the ranges to reach a Mission Hospital.

Needing a small thing seen to surgically *en route*, Rex did the job for me. I had cut open the sole of my left foot on a Balti adze when we were preparing wooden beams with which to build our school-room, and it had become painfully poisoned and badly swollen. I had to have a mountain pony for most of the journey, cutting a caper one day when I slid off its back with a splash into a river we had just forded. The brave animal had done its best to mount a steep bank. In due time Rex took a scalpel, and did the needful for my foot, a job I had done for many a Balti. On reaching Srinagar we went to our friends at the C.M.S. Hospital. Dr Norman MacPherson looked at the foot, and said, 'You are alright. He has cured you.' The sawing up of the beams for the school-room was a vain task. We never got it built. Had we done so it would all have been lost in the appalling disaster which overtook the whole valley when the icy waters of the Shyock again raged from mountain to mountain, covering homes and people with tragic loss.

A smile-raising incident happened on that journey when one evening I went out to speak to a crowd of Baltis. With all the earnestness I could command I spoke to them of the Saviour, of His love for us in dying for us upon the cross of Calvary for our salvation, and of His physical resurrection from the dead, revealing that He was God manifest in the flesh, and that now He was a for-ever-living Saviour. They appeared to listen so well and this encouraged me in the use of their speech. I was greatly surprised at the close of my talk to them when one of their number came over and said, 'Sir, we are very sorry, and regret to tell you that we do not understand English here!' A likeable young man he was. I thanked him, waved them all goodnight and went inside.

Although it was mid-summer we found ourselves crossing snows on the Zoji La and could picture in imagination what it would be like in mid-winter. At one of our camps a Kashmiri runner, carrying antlers, reached us saying that his 'shikari' (hunter) sahib was unwell and was following on two marches behind us. In due time I was to take this sick young British officer out of Srinagar to Murree, about two hundred miles, to the Military Hospital, He made the agonising journey lying on the floor of a mail-van. No wonder he appealed to the Indian driver to go slowly, often saying, 'Ahista! Ahista!' We were received at the hospital by a curt orderly who attacked me with sharp words about our time of arrival! Civilization! It made me wonder who needed evangelising! I sought out Lt. Col. Frost, in the British lines, and had prayer with him. That evening at a service I heard him make a brave witness for Christ. The unmannerly orderly was sitting near the front, and an impolite ecclesiastical dignitary was chairman who said he disagreed with what Frost would say, even before the soldier had spoken. I never heard a speaker introduced in such a way either before or since. Soon, I was to move back to the Karakoram with this to cheer me, the fearless witness of a British officer to the saving power of Jesus Christ in socalled civilization. Next day I set out for Srinagar and was soon moving on again across the Himalaya.

14: *Baltistan once more*

Before ever we had gone to Baltistan at all, Rex, in Srinagar, had a few sessions of Bible teaching with several young men and among them was Iman Admi, an athletic Kashmiri, who showed great interest in Christ and the Scriptures and became assured of salvation. Spiritually he matured quickly and expressed a wish to accompany us to the Karakoram. Well educated and intelligent he was fluent in English, Kashmiri and Urdu, and we felt that he would be a helpful member of our team. When we got to Doghoni we appointed him as headmaster of the boys' school. Though he spoke no Balti Thibetan most of the scholars had enough Urdu to understand and follow him in their lessons.

Iman Admi had been less than a year with us when he expressed his desire to be baptised, in the Name of Christ, in his native Srinagar. We were not sure that it was right and wise for this to take place where he had been brought up as a Moslem, and where his close relations and friends were Moslems. But he was determined that it should be so, and we agreed.

Now that we were again in Srinagar preparations were made for the baptism, and we conferred with fellow missionaries about the day, time and procedure. Knowing that there might be difficulties, and with Rex still unwell, we planned that Iman, Piyara and I should set off at once from Srinagar after the ceremony, cross the Wular Lake in a 'dunga' (houseboat), to Bandipura, and begin our climbs towards Baltistan. Rex, recovering from his illness, would follow later.

All was arranged. Iman and Piyara were in the centre of Srinagar City. They had been contacted, and they knew when we expected them for the baptism. That time came, but they did not. Rumours reached us that they had been roughly treated, and that an attempt would be made to stop the baptism. We waited, watched and prayed. Quite a time passed. It was decided that one of us should go to find them, and I was asked to go. Not knowing the inner city I wondered how I would fare. The Lord helped me. In a seeming maze of alley-ways I met both men coming through a doorway. Neither looked well. Iman had been drugged to prevent his being baptised. I accompanied them back in safety to where the missionaries were waiting for us. A hearty welcome they gave us. Iman was baptised, and off we went along the water canals to the Wular Lake and on to heights where we could look down on the clouds. It was said that we were being followed but we had no evidence of that. Rex stayed for treatment for his recurrence of typhoid trouble. He would come later. My last contact with Iman was by letter inviting me back to his lovely country.

We pushed on and at Burzil were held back by rains just as we had been held back the year before by snows. Coming across the Rajdiangan Pass we had an amazing view of Nanga Parbat (Naked Mountain). At Gurais some Dard ponymen joined us. To live amongst these manly chaps, in their wooden logged houses was a privilege. They are a people apart. Have they an affinity of descent from the armies of Alexander the Great? Of their language I knew nothing and do not know of anyone who does.

A fierce boil had appeared on my left knee, and a fiery one on my brow. I could not keep pace with the party. Piyara was the worse for wear, and we let him have our spare pony. He kindly let me have it now and again. Reaching the Deosai we had begun our ascent of the Sari Sungar La (14,200), when a sudden blizzard hit us. Dark clouds enveloped us, lightning flashed and thunder rolled. Hail lashed us mercilessly. My hands went numb, and I felt faint. Leaning low on the neck of the pony I called for Iman Admi who took my feet out of the rope-stirrups and lowered me down on to some cold damp stones. Resting a few minutes my faintness lifted and we moved forward. The Sari Sungar behind us, we reached our camp near Kala Pani (Black Water). From rather a line-out of stragglers Piyara was the last to arrive. He looked very tired after a most trying stormy day. It was still stormy. All we could do was to get our one tent up as soon as possible. Unloading our pack-ponies we left our yak-dhans (luggage boxes) lying in the snow which was now falling, and began to gather packs around the tent into which we crammed. What a mixture of nations! There was not enough room for all of us. Some of our ragged, lousy and flea-ridden Dards lay under the tent flaps. The others brought their quota of vermin in to us.

Bitter winds blew all night. The ponymen know how to keep warm in the smallest possible space, and we with them. I have known on the Deosai of a morning, going to what appeared to be a big round bundle of rags, encrusted with frost, tapping and pummelling it to get it to unroll to become a number of men! And to see these same people massage one another, sometimes with their feet, to help muscle tiredness, was unique, and interesting.

Getting ready in the snow we set off on a very long march at about 15,000 feet. My boil sores were worse, and my feet were now a mass of small sores which were not helped by the goatskin socks I was wearing. Piyara felt better. That cheered us. We had an encouraging reading of Scripture with him before setting out. Cold winds chilled us, although the sun shone brightly. Many a marmot came out of its den and stood up greeting us with its peculiar doglike cry, as we plodded on to our highest point, the Burji La, at 16,500 feet, which we were glad to reach. What a sight met our eyes! We stood in awe and amazement on its snow and ice, viewing mountains upon mountains, armies of mountains, their white peaks piercing the skies, and rivers of ice moving out from their chasms. Nearer to us were the villages of the Baltis lying up the valleys right to the snouts of the glaciers. Reaching the summit had been testing enough. Now the descent began on a safe-looking snowbank. We thought that we could encamp at the base of it for the night. To slide the ponies and packs down the snowy 1,500 feet or so was necessary, safe and somewhat laughable. I hobbled, slid, slithered and rolled to a level-enough place where we could set up a tent. It was a relief to get there. No other fellow-human, house, tree or bush had been seen for five or six days. Our Dards had not brought enough wood with us for our last fires! Not even enough was left to boil water for a cup of tea. Happily we had some dried apricots, dried figs and a few nuts. When I took off my skin socks my feet were an ugly sight of inflammation and pus. Things looked awkward. After all, there were four of us who had crossed into the land the year before and now there was only one of us. My feet appeared so necessary in such a land. The fiery boils on brow and knee tried me. Powers of darkness seemed to gather about, seeking to colour me within with what was without! The dismal thought came that I might get down into Baltistan, be closed in for another year by the weather, become ill and possibly die. Baltis would bury me and no one would know for a while that I had ever been there. Suddenly I thought of the words of the Saviour, 'Lo I am with you always.' In His light I saw light. Reaching for my haversack, I took out my mouth-organ and played heartily, 'From Greenland's Icy Mountains', and greatly encouraged myself in the Lord.

We had a freezing night and the ponymen brought into the tent the usual savage fleas. One of our ponies got away somewhere and could not be found. Soon it was down, down, down, from around 15,000 feet to about 8,000 feet. At times we had many a jolt. Nearing Skardu it was a cheering sight to see apricot trees, and soon, human habitations. Reaching Skardu I met a couple of travellers, Captain and Mrs Marshall. They were most

[55]

kind, helping me with my sores. They asked, 'Do you live
in this country?' I said that I did. They shook their heads,
and he said, 'If I had to live here I'd be drunk every night
so that I would not know where I was!' I said to them that
I was glad to be where the Master wanted me to be, with
the spastics, the orphans, the deaf, dumb, and mentally
deranged. How often I had seen the mentally troubled
tethered like animals to wooden posts, and to be there
lifelong. I would be happy to be shut in again for another year with Him who makes the storm a calm and
the desert to blossom as the rose. They were kind to me
and dressed my sores after I had got out my scalpel and
opened them up.

In a few days we reached Doghoni there to await the
coming of Rex, Jawani and Phru Chik. They reached us
in a week or two, well and happy. In due course, we all
set off for Shigar, there to watch and pray a time about
what we should do – all remain in the Doghoni area, or
some of us at the Shigar mission-centre which Jack
Grant and Ernest New had had to leave because of illness? It became clear that we had to part. Rex, Iman and
Phru Chik to go back to Doghoni, Piyara, Jawani and I to
remain in Shigar. A word of Scripture that greatly appealed to us was Proverbs 18:24, particularly the latter
part of it; – 'And there is a friend that sticketh closer than
a brother.' We took that friend to be the Lord Himself.
They were no sooner gone than I got down on my knees
and committed myself, and all of our work, to Him.

15: Day by day

It is a singular experience to live among a people who are removed from one's own type of civilization, culture and heritage, and to accommodate oneself to thought processes, customs, manners and demeanour, polite and colloquial language and recognised ways of approach, among varied classes of people according to their status, 'giving no offence in any thing, that the ministry be not blamed'. Living as like the people, in general, as was possible for us, we comported ourselves in human ways in the daily round and common tasks, and took part in harmless activities in order to make room for the Divine message of the Gospel. Although women and children ran into their homes to hide themselves whenever we entered villages where we were not known, the people around us knew we were approachable, and were glad of our recognition of their dignity. We had to be preserved by the Lord all the time, of course, for we were left open to peculiar surprises.

Every Balti community knows each part of the day from beginning to ending, by the light upon the mountains. One day, in Shigar, towards evening, that is, when light is upon the highest of the peaks, a young man came to talk to me about carrying my blanket, for I planned to travel to Skardu the next day. We were talking together in the stony entrance of the mission-house when he playfully put some wrestling grips upon me, and I had to respond! A wrestling match was soon in progress, with no punches given, and no word spoken. We were rather like two children at play, although my friend seemed very much in earnest! I kept wondering about the silly game I had innocently allowed to begin, yet knew that it was all a bit of Balti fun. I wondered how long I could hold out, but knew that the best result for all concerned would be that we should show ourselves matched in strength and skill. Several times I managed to bring him down, and then release him. Each time I did so he made for a stone with which to hit me! This I knew was all a part of Balti pretence, for the sake of emphasis; but taking no risks, I pounced on him again, and on we went with the battle. I had witnessed the use of a stone on a previous occasion when I dashed to the rescue of a man whom I saw threatened by another man who had raised a big stone above his head. When I urged him to put it down, he and others around said to me, smilingly, that no harm would have resulted from the use of the stone; it was merely the Balti way of emphasis in an argument!

How I wished that someone would come! I was tiring, but had to show no annoyance. I had a testimony to keep, as a friend of the people, and as a Christian among unbelievers. On we struggled; exhaustion would end it. It did! To my great relief my friend gave in. With happy smiles, and cheerful words, he went away home saying that he would call for me in the morning when the rays of the sun were on the mountain tops. He did so, and away we went together to the capital, Skardu, happy in each other's company. Our becoming all things to all men that we might win some took on some strange forms!

On one occasion, during the evening of a cold and snowy day, I learned a useful lesson. A young lad had come to my door in the afternoon, asking for clothing, and I had neglected to give anything to him. Having no underclothes and night clothes left I felt that I had given enough; but I still had garments of a kind in my yak-boxes. Silence had fallen over our deep cleft valley except for the noise of the waters. My cheering hurricane lamp was lit. Jawani was in his own part of our long mission-house, instead of sitting as he sometimes did, in our stony inner passage with a sword-like weapon upon his knees waiting for intruders. One night, hearing such a one, as he supposed, he picked up the weapon and dashed out into the entry brandishing it. Actually it was I he had heard; but I had gone through into my own part of the house before he emerged. I had been out looking for Bess, our spaniel dog. She was now asleep on some sheep-skins at the end of my string-bed. A most blessed time of the day had come, that of evening worship, but before many minutes had passed I became shamefully conscious of my refusal to help clothe the naked, and I saw what a poor representative of the Saviour I had been that day. All I had was His and when asked for clothing by the needy boy, I should have given it. If I had been in doubt I should have referred the matter to the Lord. From that evening I was enabled to do so, and often smiled in amazement, when a plea for help caused me to open my 'yak-boxes', and I began to realize what I could do without.

One morning, in the school at Shigar, a man listened, with the boys, to the Bible Lesson. We welcomed any visitor at such a time. At the close of the lesson he said to me that, unless he had been mistaken, he had heard me read that if a man had two coats he should give one of them to him who had none. I agreed that he had heard aright, and that such advice had been given by John the Baptist who prepared the way of the Lord Jesus. Our friend astonished me by saying, 'Well, you have two coats, you have one on, and I know that you have another hanging in the main room of your house, for I have seen it. What about giving me one of them?' He was surprised when I said to him, 'But that Scripture says that one of the coats should be given to him that has none. You have one on. If I give you one of mine then you will have two.' He shook his head in agreement, and said that he had never thought of that. But I had!

We lived among the people, many of them naked, vermin-ridden, sick in body and mind, bereaved and dying. Some were deranged beings, tethered to posts for life and dying comfortless. The painful pressure of sympathy was heavy upon us and we did what we could, always with the supreme aim in view of bringing to these folk the good news of salvation. We ourselves had very little of material comfort, but friends kindly sent to us useful things in small quantities. The extra finance that came, we expended on customs duties. The Baltis also brought us presents from their humble store, and would then wait for us to give them something in return, but it was far from easy to know what to give them in return!

In due time the appeal of the orphans and the constraining love of Christ compelled Rex and Julie Bavington after their marriage to open their home to all who came. The dirty, the diseased and the starving came, one lad being found lying not far from the door, only to die later. Another was deaf and dumb. Loving hands tended them, feeding, cleaning and clothing them, and teaching them about the Lord Jesus Christ. Among them was a girl named Sikimbi who arrived in a shocking condition of vermin and sores, one sore taking up most of the crown of the head. She sat in a corner, and would not speak or take part in any activity. But as the days passed she became a bright and playful little thing, anxious to accomplish small tasks. She became interested in the Saviour, and the Holy Scriptures, and expressed herself so. Some heard of this, and shortly, relations unheard of before, came along claiming her, asking that they might take her away with them. She would not go, pleading that she did not know them, and they went away without her. Sometime later, when she was in the open not far away, she never returned to the Mission House. Inquiries and search produced no results. She had been taken away, and was kept away. In Central Asia there are many chains upon its peoples put by one who himself will yet be chained, 'that is, the devil.'

We longed and prayed for a hearing ear and an understanding heart among the people, but there was much dulness of hearing and darkness of understanding among them. Often disgust was expressed at the Name which is above every name in heaven and earth, and at which every knee shall bow. It was heard with horror, obnoxious spitting and the throwing up of hands in disapproval. Sometimes as we spoke the Gospel of Christ in the dispensary it was not well received. A man clapped his hands over his ears, and said he could not hear! 'Kwa mit!' he said, 'Kwa mit!' 'I cannot hear! I cannot hear!' Another turned to him and said, 'You can hear; he is speaking our language!' Dissent was recorded! 'I mean that I do not want to hear or understand, in my heart.' He placed a hand upon his breast.

16: *Clarke Sahib*

Coming round a corner of a house in Skardu, near the junction of the Indus and the Shigar Rivers, I met, face to face, a Britisher. A yard or two this way or that, a minute or two earlier or later, would have made a vital difference, and we would never have met. We asked the same question of each other, 'Hullo! Who are you?' The one said, 'My name is Captain Clarke of the Royal Engineers, and I am hunting.' The other said, 'My name is Purves and I am a missionary of the Gospel in Baltistan.' Captain Clarke looked at me incredulously. 'A missionary,' he said, 'in these parts?' There were a few more exchanges of conversation and we parted.

Some years later I was on my way to Aldershot to speak at an Officers Christian Union meeting. It was the O.C.U. who paid my passage to the Mission Field, supplied my equipment, and supported me for a year, from moneys generously given by a fine Christian man in South Africa, the late Captain Dobbie. I was glad of fellowship with any of its members. A lady kindly met me as I left the train, and in the course of conversation, while on the way to the hall, I asked her the name of the chairman of the meeting. She smiled, saying that she was told not to tell me, and that I would be much surprised when I saw him. Surprise! Delightful surprise indeed! I could hardly believe my eyes! It was Captain Clarke of the Balti house-corner in Skardu! And to meet each other again at a Christian missionary meeting, and he in the chair leading it; it was wonderful indeed!

Speaking with him before the service began I mentioned to him that when we had met in Baltistan he did not give me the impression that he was a Christian. He agreed that that was a true impression, but that from the time of that unexpected meeting, he had begun to think about himself and his life in a new way, and could not but contrast his purpose in making an expensive trip to the Karakoram for his own pleasure, and returning again to civilisation and its comforts, with the very different purpose of a person living in these inhospitable regions, summer and winter, as a missionary of the Gospel. 'I decided,' he said, 'that on returning to my unit in India, whenever I had the opportunity of going to a Gospel service, I would go and make an open confession of Christ. This I did. And here I am, Purves, leading the meeting for you tonight.' And what an enthusiastic leader he was! In some ways I was sorry that I had to speak. He spoke of the Saviour, and of our unexpected meeting, of Lesser Thibet, and of the spiritual and social needs of its people. It was inspiring to listen to him. He has long been interested in the evangelising of Central Asia, and has worked much towards that great end. He is, at the time of writing, Lieut. Colonel G. C. S. Clarke, D.S.O., O.B.E., Chairman of the Central Asian Mission, and has been a prominent member of the Officers Christian Union. Having been loaned by The Worldwide Evangelization Crusade to the Central Asian Mission for one or two years I know something of its noble work among Islamic peoples. It was founded by Colonel G. and Mrs Wingate, the parents of the late 'Chindit' Wingate, and of the late Miss Rachel Wingate, sometime missionary in Kashgar, Chinese Turkestan. I was privileged to know the family, who encouraged me in the Lord and in missionary work.

17: A couple in Skoro

All day I had been away from Shigar, and feeling very tired I was returning home. Living never below 8,000 feet, one was sometimes tired. Selfishly, I hoped that no-one in need would be waiting for me. But such there appeared to be. I could see him standing at the Mission House door, a youngish Balti, seemingly quite distressed. Slowly reaching him I exchanged greetings, and he appealed to me to go with him to see his wife, who was ill. I could not make out from him what the trouble was, but it was evident that she was in urgent need of help. 'You must go with me,' he said. On asking him where his home was he told me it was in the village of Skoro, near the Skoro La. It was on the edge of the unexplored. The journey would take us hours into the night. Feeling my own physical disability I told the man that I could not go until the next day. His face fell, and I felt ashamed. My conscience would not clear, and I knew that I needed to pray about going or staying. Asking the Skoropa, (man from Skoro) to wait a little, I said that I would shortly give him my answer. Going into my room I knelt down by my string-bed, and asked the Lord Jesus to give me assurance about what I should do. In a few minutes I knew I had to go, and said so to the Skoropa. He was delighted.

Gathering a few necessary things together – bandages, gauze, lint, cottonwool, scissors, scalpels, and so on, we set off trudging along the narrow mountain paths. A brilliant moon was bathing everything in a silver radiance, and the sparkling, starry, gem-studded sky above us seemed to be so near. Mighty waters thundered and boomed their swift and deep ways, foaming over the rocks to be lost in the chasms. My friend with me I liked very much. I knew he was anxious; but it was evident he hoped I could help. Reaching Skoro we hurriedly passed up through its moonlit narrow passages, and coming to a reed-woven wicker door he pushed it open. All tiredness had left me. I knew that I was on an errand of His mercy. We entered a dimly-lit room where reed wicks burned in small stone cups of melted butter ('mar' – the same word is used for butter and oil). A wood fire burned in the middle of the floor. A huddled figure of a young woman sat near it, and the slow moving figure of an elderly woman came towards us. My friend went to the woman by the fire, got down beside her, put an arm around her and said to her, 'See dear, I have brought the European to see you. He will help you.' I admired him. The man within me was for him. I went over and they showed me what was wrong. Her right breast was in an agonising condition with pus oozing from it. She looked extremely ill; dirty too, and the stench from her condition was nauseating. All power to help herself was gone, and she was worn to a shadow. It was strange to feel that one was in a part of the world where there was neither nurse nor doctor. I did not know what to do. My supply of chloroform was finished. Not knowing what to do became wondering what to do. Telling the husband I would return soon I went outside. The air was icy chilled, but I had to wipe the perspiration from my brow. Jagged snowy peaks stood out against the moonlit purple sky. Mount Godwin Austen was comparatively near. Our world was that only of mountains. I prayed, asking God to help me to help the poor suffering Skoropang-o, and her splendid husband, and said that I was willing to take the scalpel and lance the breast if He would give me assurance that I was doing the right and safe thing. That assurance came in a moment. Going inside the humble home again I said to the husband, that I would like to speak to him. We went aside and I told him what had to be done, and asked him to speak to Api (grandmother) and take her into our confidence. He and she were to support his wife in their arms when all was ready. First, they had to get a warmer fire burning, for which they had no fuel but wood, dried leaves and apricot kernel shells. They soon had a brighter glow showing. For lighting fires the Baltis use the flint and tinder, or a glowing ember from a neighbour's fire. They have no matches. We had no light that early morning except that from the 'ot' (stone crusie) with its floating wool wick in the melted butter. Some water was boiled for us to wash her with. I had a piece of soap, a scarce commodity locally, and known in Urdu as 'savon' from the French. As we washed her the stench was overpowering and horrid lice were crawling over my hands and arms as we worked. Time and again I swathed them off. It was a nauseating task.

Getting more boiling water for my scalpel in my useful enamel dish, I asked the Skoropa and Api, to take Bong-o (sister) firmly in their arms. Sterilising the hidden knife I cut at what appeared to be the weakest part of the breast wall, from which the pus was oozing out. Quickly I dropped the scalpel, picked up the dish which I had ready, and held it till it was full of pus. Bong-o lay back faint and helpless in her husband's arms. As cleanly as possible I bandaged her up after plugging the wound with gauze. Lice! Lice! And more lice! The horror of them! They made one sick. And then as we sat around the smoky fire, I read to them, and spoke to them about the Lord Jesus Christ of whom they had not heard before.

After prayer I took my way again among the great silences of these early hours before 'go-bya,' or 'the first crowing of the cock.' Soon there would be the 'skil bya,' which is 'the second crowing of the cock', and then the 'juk-bya,' or 'the last crowing of the cock', herald of the dawn. But I broke these silences with my merry singing, and coming to a broad piece of the path I hung my haversack on a jagged bit of rock and imitated King David! I was so happy.

Some hours of rest and I returned to see my new friends, and did so again and again to clean and help her. Soon Bong-o got stronger and was on her feet once more. Her cheeks filled out and a bit of colour came to them. The wound healed, and once more she was the wife and mother, a happy lass, in her own humble Karakoram home. It was pleasing to see their gratitude but out of their generous poverty I could accept little. And always there was the sitting around the fire, the troublesome smoke making its way, as best it could, through a hole in the rafters as we read and spoke about the greatest subject in the world, the Lord Jesus Christ and His salvation.

18: Zafar my friend

The Baltis are a kindly people; and most of them have a humble opinion of themselves, realising their lack of education, and their poverty of everything that goes to make life worth while. I have known Baltis quite apologetic about themselves, even to saying, 'You must think that we are animals.' I assured them that I did nothing of the kind, that I liked them, admired them, and was delighted to live among them. There were the exceptions. Some maybe, out of the hardness of their own lives, were inclined to be hard on animals. Horses and cattle were worked far too heavily. Donkeys became skin and bone through sparse feeding, and pet animals suffered when families fell out with each other. Never liking cruelty in any form, I met with difficulties in defence of the beasts of the field and the home.

I got into trouble with a certain Zafar Gopa. Meeting one of his servants driving some boney donkeys before him, and threateningly wielding a heavy stick over them, I feared that if he used it the poor 'bong-bung-kun' might be painfully injured. Speaking to him I showed him how dangerous it could be for the creatures if he used such an implement on them. Jokingly I took the cudgel from him gave him a playful poke with it, and we both had a laugh. Saying cheerio to each other I urged him to get a thin wand for the 'bong-bung-kun.'

Later the same day Jawani informed me that one of the Rajah's chief men was at the door. He wanted to see me, and he did not seem very pleased. I went to the door, and invited him in. It was Zafar Gopa! He was a man who had never once looked pleasantly at me. Now he was in a violent temper, accusing me of having attacked his 'bizba,' (servant) who looked after his donkeys, and that he was now lying in his house hardly able to move. I pointed out to him that either he or his worker was telling lies. On he stormed telling me what he thought of me, nor did I like it for I was innocent of his charges. He refused to listen to me, but stormed on about what was to happen to me, ending with the threat that he would bring me before the chief ruler of the country. Pleased that he had come to such a decision I told him that this was splendid, and that I would be glad to stand in their courts, and make a plea for the beasts of burden in the land. With that I politely asked him to go. He refused to go, but stood defiantly pouring out what he felt about me. Again I asked him to go, telling him that he had made his decision about me, and that it was only right that he should leave my home as I requested. Not so, Zafar! I took a step towards him and he took a step backwards! Forward! Backward! Forward! Backward! To the door! And the next moment he was running across the 'polo-jing,' and I was running after him. I did not want to catch him. I returned to my 'nangnu' feeling a bit foolish. I had tarnished my witness for the Master and His cause. Only two Europeans in the land, both missionaries, and four days of up-and-down travel between them! Both surrounded by people of another faith! I thought I heard the devil laugh! There was only one thing to do. Confess it all to the Lord and go forward trusting Him.

Some hours later Piyara Dost came in. He was laughing, and evidently much amused about some happening. Asking him why, I was told that Zafar was up in Shigar Bazaar and was telling a story there of how Jan Sahib had chased him with a revolver and nearly shot him! 'Oh, Piyara,' I said, 'I do not see very much to laugh at in all of this. It is quite distressing to me.' Piyara laughed the more, treating the affair as a joke. It would be something to talk about, pass comment on, and consider the whys and wherefores of, in many a conversation for some time to come. In a land where even a bicycle bell was never heard, until my fellow-missionary brought a bicycle in, such an incident could become a welcome event.

When I used to meet him, Zafar wore a more distasteful scowl than ever. I tried smiling to him, but all to no avail. I would have apologised to him, but for the refuge of lies in which he was hiding. But a very welcome and happy surprise came my way. Jawani came in to say that Zafir Gopa was again at my door and wished to speak with me. Out I went, and invited him in. What a change! He was so quietly spoken, polite and apologetic, saying that he wanted forgiveness for all that he had said, and that he had told lies about me, and was now ever so sorry, for he knew that he had wronged me. 'You are our friend,' he said. 'You help everybody. I, Zafar, wish to be your friend, and to help you.' Gladly I accepted his apology, and made my own to him. I said that it was truly manly of him, and I admired him for coming to me. 'I shall ever be a friend of yours,' he told me, 'and if ever you need someone to help you, send for me.' Until I left the Shigar Valleys, Zafar Gopa was a true friend. There was never a sneer or scowl again from him, only glad and happy smiles. This meant much to me in a place where the loving kindness of God in Christ was not known, but to which one was bearing witness every day. Alas, no one is there now that we know of, to preach Christ and His 'karo-shing' (cross); nor has there been for years! Will there ever be again?

19: *Who? What? When? Where?*

Who? What? When? Where?, or as the Baltis would say, 'Su? Chi? Nam? Gar?', meant much to us day and night. Such questions and the answers given them were parts of the stuff of our lives, wherever we travelled or stayed; and also when we met after being months apart, and could hardly recognise each other. At the rendezvous I might say to a strange figure, 'bearded like the pard,' (leopard) of which we had a unique and beautiful variety, and hoped for its protection, 'Is that you, Rex?' How cheering to hear the welcome reply, 'Yes, is that you, Jock?'

What fellowship we had together, and many a hearty laugh as on one occasion when we slept on the floor of a Rest House, and had a Balti friend with us. Our laugh was about the way he lay down for his night's rest. He simply divested himself of all that he wore, and covered himself then with all of his garments. No wonder Baltis travelled lightly! It was cheering to see how comfortable a position he got himself into, while outside around the house vultures, like yelping dogs, uttered their strange cries. We ourselves went to rest with a change of Balti outfit as strange as we wore by day.

If overtaken by darkness we stayed where we were. A false step, and we would have disappeared for ever. Narrow ledges, high up on precipice sides compelled us, except under brilliant moonlight, to wait for the day. One chilly night was tiring and trying. After reaching a travellers' stopping place, we tried in all sorts of ways to keep warm during the night, even to folding ourselves in each other's arms, but without success. Up we got and joined the warming heat of the Baltis who were with us, and became part of the bundle with them. It meant a fresh invasion of lice, of which we had plenty already, and could put our hands behind our necks, and pull them out in the palms of our hands. Deadly things! A neighbourly pastime of Balti women, as they sat in the sun, on their flat rooftops, was vermin hunting in each other's head of hair. And, alas, it has to be said, sometimes one could see certain women take them between their teeth. Exaggeration! Not at all. And so trying was the vermin to us that we had nightmares in which our heads appeared to us as deep Karakoram valleys filled with lice!

House-bugs were hideous things, and the smell from them nauseating. Never having seen them until we lived in Doghoni, we wondered what the reddish creatures were which dropped on us and on our beds from the rafters above. Their bites were like jabs from an electric needle. They made us ill. Living as we did among the people we just could not keep clean, and one of our last jobs at night was running along the seams of our undergarments, when we had such, with a lighted candle. When we washed our clothes, and hung them out to dry, they were like frozen boards, with the vermin on them like ears of barley. For us there was no protection, as we worked day and night among the people in need, the sick and the dying.

One day, Jawani came into the Mission House, saying that a strange-looking man with big glassy eyes was at the door wanting to see me. I went out, and there was Rex! Big eyed indeed because of his spectacles, on his black-bearded face. What a joyous time we had far into the night! We actually opened two tins of our emergency rations, and with a few 'chapati' (unleavened cakes), tinned butter, syrup and tea, it was all a feast indeed.

How interesting it was recounting to each other our experiences of the Lord, His Word, His guidance, encounters and blessings since last we had seen each other. Many of our favourite hymns we sang together, such as, 'I know of a world that is sunk in shame,' and, 'Still, still with Thee when purple morning breaketh when the bird waketh, and the shadows flee;' and 'Mhirban, Mhirban, Mhirban,' or 'Kind, Friendly and Gracious.' I had my accordion and Rex took down my mantelshelf, a kerosene tin shaped that way, to play on as a drum. We were the happiest young men in the world.

His visit was unexpected, and he told me the reason for it. It was to ask me to accompany him to Ladakh, Western Thibet. He had proposed marriage to Miss Julie Trumpler, of the Central Asian Mission, working there with her colleague, Miss Eliza Messaz, both then serving with the Moravians. Miss Messaz became the wife of Mr Alfred Read of the C.A.M. He knew the Balti tongue as none of us ever knew it, compiling both a grammar and dictionary. One cannot speak too highly of their work. They hazarded their lives for the Gospel's sake in the high places of the field. Happy to go with my fellow-workers, Jawani, and Phru Chik, whom Rex had brought with him, we set off for Doghoni to go from there to Ladakh, Western Thibet. I would not be back again in Shigar for months, during which my times of sleeping in a bed would be rare indeed.

So it was Shigar to Doghoni, to Kuru, Kiris, Parkutta, Tolti and Kharmang, and *en route* one fine morning we heard one of the finest renderings of the muezzin we ever heard in Central Asia. At dawn with stars yet twinkling, and while we still lay on the ground, a mullah sang his fascinating rendering of the Muslim call to prayer. He was somewhere near but unseen. None of us spoke until he finished. My colleague had listened as I had. The stars paled, and Jawani and Phru Chik soon had the camp-fire burning, with short bright flames shooting up among the shadows of the tall thin trees. Here and there, as we went on our way, we talked with some about the Saviour, and gave portions of Scripture to anyone who said he could read, or would be able to have someone who could read to him. Where the Shyock joined the Indus we crossed on the familiar 'zach,' (raft of inflated goatskins). Vegetables could not be obtained. The usual disappointing answer to our request for them was, 'All have been used up.' But we did get a few in one place in exchange for some pills, and were glad too, to exchange the latter for some wild nettles. Not a leaf or a crust of bread is knowingly wasted in Baltistan . . . On we went towards Kharmang.

All went well on our journey, apart from a few minor happenings, till we reached the giant trapeze, the 'zamba-thaqpa' (rope-bridge) stretched across the foaming, roaring Indus at Kharmang. Then the unexpected began to happen. A strong wind blew down the deep ravine. Heavy clouds gathered. I would rather it had remained calm! We had planned to cross the bridge into quite unknown country, seeking a shorter way into Ladakh, and had no knowledge of any European ever having crossed it before. It swung in the wind, all its seventy yards or so, like a sort of spider-web. About sixty feet below were the jagged rocks, and the swirling waters of the Indus. Because of the thunder of them we had to shout into each other's ears. 'Maybe this is the Glory day,' Rex said to me.

The bridge was made of four strong wire ropes; two were joined closely together to tightrope on, and one for each hand to hold on to. Very widely set were willow wands pleated around them, and underneath them. Baltis were on the other side of the river, and finally, by shouting our loudest, we managed to make them hear us, asking if the bridge was safe to cross. Back came the halloed and valley-echoing answer, 'If God wills.' So flimsy looking amid immensities of nature the 'zamba' swung up and down. Phru Chik sat on the rocks staring at it and at the leaping waters. But what of Bess, our spaniel dog? Our first plan for her crossing was that we should tie her legs and Rex would carry her across, slung around his neck. But we soon saw that such an idea was impracticable, and, indeed, dangerous. The slightest imbalance on the wire strands might send man and dog plunging into the torrents below. We decided to tie her up in towels, and suitably reward a Balti for carrying her across in a back-basket, interestingly enough called a 'kari.' Phru Chik continued to look at the raging waters. Rex got busy tying up Bess. He would have wanted to go first but he did not see me mount the rocky parapet and set out on the only tightrope walking I have ever done. Out over the foam-sprayed rocks, and deep sliding waters, my world began to turn upside down as the ropes lifted and fell, and I was lifted seemingly to the sky, and down again, to meet the rocks and the waters, and join their crash with the whistling of the winds, which swung one up on one's side to the left and then, as the ropes fell, to the right. Out on the bridge a fair distance I thought of turning back, feeling that I would never get to the other side, when suddenly there came into mind a few words of a hymn, 'When I fear my faith would fail, He will hold me fast.' 'When I fear! . . . My faith would fail! . . . He will hold me fast!' Faith triumphed! On I went, hand by hand, one only at a time, and never moving a hand when I moved a foot. The winds whistled round me. I was swinging about in a great Karakoram valley above one of the world's mightiest rivers. Then I began to move up the ropes towards the end of the bridge. Baltis kindly kept looking down at me giving me advice on how to place my feet, and one of them bravely came down the ropes to keep closed hand-ropes apart for me. At one point a foot slipped and I held on grimly with both hands and the other foot.

Rex waited till I was safely over before he set out. I hoped he would be as fortunate as I had been with only a small injury to one of my hands. Jawani, barefooted, came next, after seeking a word of promise from the New Testament. 'See how dry my lips are,' he said, as he joined us on the rocks above. Phru Chik just would not cross, and we signalled and shouted to him to move farther up the valley, where, we were told, there was a raft of some kind by which he could be ferried over to us. Bess was safely brought over to us in the 'kari'.

Months later I was speaking to a military hunter quite near the bridge. As we looked at it he asked me if I had ever crossed it, and I said that I had done so. 'What,' he said! 'I would not put a foot on it. And if I had the power to do so, I would give you a V.C.!' I told him about the three of us going over. He asked me to go on it again so that he could take a photograph. I declined, saying that I would do so in the course of my missionary duties! But going on it for the sake of a picture was like tempting providence. He agreed!

Very little rain ever falls in Baltistan, but that day some did fall and we left our 'zamba-thaqpa' swaying dismally in it as we moved on up the valley, towards Kharmang. Speaking with some Baltis about the way we intended to take next day, they shook their heads disapprovingly saying that it meant grave danger to life and limb. Missionaries were strange people to them. They apparently took us for some sort of explorers or hunters. There is no record that I know of, of any European having been there among them before. A band of them convinced us that we should not go on our proposed way and they accompanied us up the river side to await the raft on which Phru Chik was to cross to us. They advised us to go across to him instead.

There were signals and shoutings, and as we sat in the rain, suddenly we saw a figure standing stride-legs on some kind of craft being propelled towards us. It was evident that the figure knew the river and its currents, for he whirled his frail looking thing this way and that way, a master in his element. When he reached us I almost greeted him as 'Robinson Crusoe.' Only one of us at a time could be ferried across with him. Jawani being cook, went first; Rex went next, because he had a sore throat, and because he had on a well-soaked garment. Bess went with him. Baltis are a likeable people, but I had an uncanny feeling of insecurity and aloneness that day as I stood among that group speaking to them about the Saviour, and was glad when I got on to the raft, and was spinning away into the eddies of the Indus. My steersman, about mid-river, took a happy and foolish turn, feeling, I think, that his task was nearly over. He began to show his prowess on the river by spinning his craft round and round! The merry rogue watched me as he did so. He was trying to scare me, and laughed heartily when I said to him, 'It's all right! Remember you too are on this raft!'

Reaching the rocky shore I made for the village of Bagicha, where I found my fellow-missionary seated, and drying his shirt at the camp-fire. With their tutor, two young sons of the local Rajah came to see us, and after talking with us they accepted copies of Gospels. Under the stars that night we lay down in a place we had not expected to be in, Bagicha (garden).

Now, we were on the trail for Olthing Thang and Kargil. Away across the Indus we could see the thin path we would have taken had we gone on from Kharmang. Sometimes it reared up like a ladder placed against a house, and dived away down again until it seemed to be in the bed of the river; and then away up, and up, until it disappeared. On asking my colleague where he thought it was, he said, in Balti, that it had flown away! It was the last we saw of it. We thought that we might make for the houses of Marol perched high among the crags; but from our own high vantage point we could see that it would hold no extra supplies for us. We met a group of descending Baltis, who told us not to attempt to climb to Marol, and imitated what the way there was like, by crawling on their hands and knees. Short cuts in the Himalaya and Karakoram are usually misleading.

The dwellings of Olthing Thang finally came into view, and we stayed there over the weekend, and kept Sunday as a day unto the Lord in prayer and reading of the Scriptures. From the great rocks above one could look down into 600 ft chasms, and see the Suru River rushing along in its deep and tumultuous flow, lashing itself with a thunderous boom against the high canyon walls. It fascinated me to lie on safe precipice edges far above and listen to it as it sped on its course to make the mighty Indus mightier still. On we travelled to cosmopolitan Kargil, a crossroads of Central Asian people – Ladakis, Baltis, Kashmiris, Thibetans, Turkis, Punjabis, all of them members of various religions – Buddhists, Moslems, Hindus and Parsees. Any Christians? We met none at all. It was here, later, that I hoped to meet the Misses Cable and French when they essayed to return to China. But a Government order was not granted to them. There, we ourselves waited for a permit from the British Resident in Srinagar for us to move up into Ladakh where we were to be privileged to meet Yoseb Gergen whose manuscripts passed up and down through this interesting township, those manuscripts of his great and good work of the translation of the Word of God, the Holy Scriptures, into Thibetan. While there, a lad said to us that he certainly wanted to have a holy heart, and would read the booklet of Scriptures we gave him. And there we met the first European we had seen for months. As usual, a hunter.

20: *In Yoseb Gergen country*

The day after our permit arrived in Kargil, for us to journey into Ladakh, we set out while the stars were still shining, for the land of the lamas, and reached one of the farthest western points of Lamaistic Buddhism, the township of Shergol. Some refreshing springs of water were gushing there, 'lachmo grachno chhu,' as the Baltis say, 'cold and good water!' Then we saw an unaccustomed sight, and picturesque too, the whitened 'chhortens,' the repositories of the ashes of the dead, like huge bells in shape, sounding out their message, as it were, to the Thibetan Buddhist on his way to Nirvana. How delightful it was to drink from a spring, a 'chhu mik,' or 'an eye of water', as the Baltis so beautifully term it. We went on to Mulbeck Chamba, with its Gompa (monastery) standing sheer on the heights above. As we pitched our tents on the polo-ground, I was surprised by a youth hurrying towards me, and saying very enthusiastically, in English, 'Good-bye, sir.' No doubt he meant to wish me a good afternoon. He was a Kashmiri Moslem, and the village schoolmaster. We talked with him about the Saviour and the Holy Scriptures.

Next, came our crossing of the Namika La, an easy enough ascent at around 13,000 feet. Statues of the Buddha were to be seen here and there, including a very high one cut out of the solid rockface of a cliff. We were now quite often meeting 'Red Hat' and 'Yellow Hat' Lamas besides Lamaistic nuns. Prayer-flags and prayer wheels were everywhere. My left ankle had swollen badly from the weakness of an old sprain, and I was allowed a mountain pony all to myself. While I was bathing the foot in an ice-cold crystal stream an old man sat on the opposite bank turning, ever turning his prayer-wheel, quite oblivious to my strange presence. How beautifully carved in the stones of the prayer-walls were the lotus flower, and the prayer, both in Sanskrit and Thibetan lettering, 'Om Mani Padme Hum'! Could we interpret it as ignorant worship of 'The Unknown God'? An old man came wanting to sell us a bowl, which he said, was made in Lhasa. Of that we could not be sure, but we could not afford what he asked for it. All the time he kept counting his beads, made of bone and animal shell. The bowl was well enough made from wood. The Baltis actually make waterpots cut out of stone. One was in the missionhouse, but someone with a liking for it, had taken it away.

The pony I had was a strong mount and could gallop happily along the trails. I let him free when ascending, and curbed his eagerness when descending. As usual, I had a pack on my back, happily so, for while careering along a mountain side, and not having any stirrups, and only a native-made saddle to sit on, covered by a blanket, I went shooting off his back into the dust. Landing back on my pack, I suffered only a few scratches, though one of his hooves hit my right knee. No harm was done. Off he went down a valley, but Jawani went to get him for me before we crossed the Phutu La. On we went to Lama-yuru, a fantastic town of lamaseries and nunneries piled high, then higher, and so to the limit! It was refreshing to sit and have a drink at an 'eye of water,' and take a bite of food. We enjoyed talking to both Buddhists and

Moslems about the great subject of salvation, seeking to show them that it was only in and by the Lord Jesus Christ that we had forgiveness of sin.

By this time we were now near Khalatse, Ladakh, and the Moravian Mission House, occupied by humble and faithful missionaries, Mr and Mrs Kunick, true representatives of the Herrnhut Fellowship of which Thomas Chalmers wrote so glowingly, and about which much could be said in its thrilling missionary endeavours. The lady-missionaries, Miss Julie Trumpler and Miss Eliza Messaz, of the Central Asia Mission, were resident with the Kunicks. What a welcome we had, especially Rex, who had come to speak with Julie Trumpler, his bride-to-be.

It was a joy, too, to meet Mr Jack Matthewson, who with the missionary Mr V. G. Phymire, and a German scientist, had crossed Thibet from North West China. A missionary of the China Inland Mission, now the Overseas Missionary Fellowship, Jack Matthewson later served a number of years on the Home Staff of the Worldwide Evangelization Crusade, in Australia. They had had to enter Thibet from China, to find safety from rebel forces, thinking that they might reach our part of the country in four months, but it took them ten. One of the reasons for this was that they were captured by brigands, and held for several months. When they came towards our part of the Himalaya Jack's feet became badly frostbitten. The other two men were able to press on southwards to civilisation. It is a trying thing to see anyone's toes severely eaten away by frostbite as Jack's were. We found him to be a prayerful man, and with him we enjoyed fellowship in the Gospel. As for ourselves, staying at Khalatse, hours were spent every day learning to read Thibetan lettering which our Baltis did not know.

The trek from Khalatse towards Leh meant rocky paths, silver sands, and 'willows by the water-courses,' bell-like 'chhortens' by the wayside, 'gompas' on the cliffs, prayer-wheels and prayer-flags, red and yellow lamas, workaday lamaistic nuns, and interesting, pleasant people to meet and talk to as we passed through the townships of Nurla, Saspul, Bazgo, Nimu and Pitak, all built beside tributaries running swiftly into the Indus. The 'gompa' at Pitak, up on a huge rock, appeared to be in a ruinous condition. The remains of a fort, massive enough, were close by, but bore no comparison with Leh Castle, which we were soon to see, with the Moslem mosque, which rather jarred our sensibilities, in its shadow. Soon we were to hear from it the tuneful calls to prayer claiming that there is no God but Allah and Muhammad is his messenger. With some of that persuasion we talked about Him from the heart of God who had wonderfully declared the Most High to the world. With others of the Noble Eightfold Path we also talked. We seemed to be making an impression on them only to find that it was like pressing a rubber ball which came out to its own shape again. By contrast the Moslem was usually hard, and thought it wrong even to listen to us.

What a meeting place of religions and races was the spacious bazaar of Leh! And polo was sometimes played in the streets! We rubbed shoulders and exchanged greetings with Ladakhis, Thibetans, Baltis, Kashmiris, Turkis, Punjabis, Pathans, and others, but met no Europeans except a German Moravian missionary. To all alike we bore Christian witness.

Dr Redslob and Dr Marx, sometime Moravian missionaries in Leh, died of that strange disease known as Ladakhi Fever, the one the one day, and the other the next. It is a kind of Typhus or Typhoid Fever prevalent in

Central Asia, the same one that had previously attacked my colleague. Nursing him I had wondered if he would recover. As I stood at the small memorial slabs lying in the stony earth of Ladakh I had uplifting thoughts of Count Zinzendorf, the Moravian Revival, the Hundred Years' Prayer Meeting, Böhler and John Wesley in Aldersgate Street Meeting, the spiritual songs of Montgomery, Cennick, and others, and the enthusiastic surge of missionary enterprise, in one of the finest epics of church history.

Both Redslob and Marx were scholars in Thibetan language and culture, who worked very hard to give the people of Thibet the Bible in their own tongue. Yet, as I stood at that memorable spot, lamas in a nearby 'gompa' were blowing their long horns as if to say that the kingdoms of this world were not yet become the kingdoms of the Lord and of his Christ. But, not far away, there was encouragement beyond the telling. 'Yoseb Gergen the Translator,' as he is deservedly named, was a true son of his people till the end. I met him seated at his great task, revising the portion of scripture which had already been translated into Thibetan. This was to fit in with his complete translation of the whole, a task which took him thirty-five years. It is a story of loving devotion to the Lord Jesus Christ and His cause, ably told by Chandu Ray of the British and Foreign Bible Society, India, who printed the Thibetan Bible, and one of the most thrilling stories of missionary endeavour of the twentieth century. At one stage of the work, we are told, 'Yoseb Gergen undertook to write out the whole Bible by hand. He worked day and night . . . He may live five days or five months. There is a fire burning in him that is keeping him alive!' It is a moving and thrilling account of a man's love for His Saviour and his people, giving his all for them that

[83]

they might have the word of salvation. On two occasions sets of proofs were ruined and lost in the mountain passes, and the brave bringing of the third and last set of corrected proofs all the way from Leh to Lahore by a Ladakhi Christian fills one with moving admiration, with praise and thanks to God for the preservation of the carrier and the priceless manuscripts. One who met Gergen says of him, 'He was a man who truly deserved the name of Christian, for never have I come across anyone in whom the love of Christ, and the imitation of His life were more manifest. There was no attempt to slur over the inconvenient portions of Christ's teaching; in him was the simplicity of a child, side by side with the wisdom of a cultivated, well-informed mind. We always spoke of him as Gergen the Translator, . . . a man who tried only to impart to others a doctrine which he had first practised himself.' Yoseb Gergen died a few days after his work was completed. He never saw a published copy of the Bible in Thibetan. Going to the British and Foreign Bible Society headquarters, in London, to see a copy I was allowed to hold it in my hands on its being taken out of its glass case. My heart filled with praise to God.

Mahayana, 'the Great Way of Supreme Compassion,' is the Buddhism of Thibet, and according to its tenets, by practising it, anyone may become a 'buddha,' an 'enlightened one,' bringing compassion to himself and radiating it to the universe. A 'mantra' is a sound in the form of one or more syllables representing an aspect of the universe, and the greatest 'mantra' of all is 'awm' or 'om' which is thought to be the sound of the essence of all things, or the gods, as some interpret it. The most familiar and most used 'mantra' is 'Om mani padme hum,' meaning 'O jewel in the lotus.' There is also the 'mandala,' the symbolic picture of an aspect, or aspects, of the universe and the human mind which should be visualised with the repetition of the 'mantra.'

The novice in Mahayana has to develop his inner seeing powers by the use of easily understood images, of which none can compare with the lotus, the premier symbol, for him, of the enlightenment of the human mind, and also its perfect unfolding. Its roots (bodily existence) are buried deep in the nourishing earth and mud, and its bloom or flower (the enlightened mind) rises above the water, and opens out into immensity, symbolic of the act of spiritual unfolding, with the urge of the seed always to grow (the human mind always transcending itself). Fully opened the lotus is the supreme symbol of the Buddha mind, the mind that knows the true nature of existence.

The six syllables of 'Om Mani Padme Hum,' represent the six worlds of Thibetan Buddhism, and each of them represents a state or condition of the mind of man. They are often set forth in colourful and graphic picture form, perceiving which, the devotee sees himself and his universe as he intones the 'mantra.' Slowly intoned, and directed outwards they send forth helpful compassion to the Mahayana worlds, and generate compassion to him who prays. The written form of each syllable is believed to give rays of comfort to the beings of the worlds – Om, the highest of beings; Ma, demons; Ni, humans; Pad, animals; Me, wandering spirits; and Hum, hell, the experience and state of the tortured mind. In Mahayana Buddhism the greatest 'mandala' of all is that of 'The Wheel of Life.' Here are 'The Six Worlds,' or states of continuous becoming. A terrible monster, Yama, the Lord of Death, signifying foolish, vain, and cruel deluded desires of mankind, holds them all in his ghastly and fearsome grip. The compassionate Buddha, who is depicted in each of the parts of the wheel tendering his help, and outside the Wheel appears on rainbow tinted clouds, points out the Way to spiritual illumination and freedom from bondage.

21: *Himalaya travels*

Cheerily we moved out of Leh, caravan centre and one of the most highly placed towns on earth, en route for Srinagar, Kashmir, and the intended marriage of Rex and Julie at which I had been asked to be best man. I did not know at that time that I would be a fortnight late for the wedding! The members of our party with them were Eliza Messaz, Jack Matthewson, Jawani, Phru Chik and myself. Jack's feet were now recovering from the frostbite but had to be dressed daily. But there were times when he liked to dismount and we would sit with him, our backs against the rocks, read a little of the Word, and talk about the Saviour and His ways with us. Jack was carried on the back of a fine horse called Makhmal (Velvet).

We reached once more the hobgoblin-looking town of Yuru, better known as the lamaistic town of Lamayuru. Its setting in a hollow of the hills is unforgettable, with its massive red sandstone cliffs holed with many caves, rising high above the town. Its lines of Mani prayer walls and chhortens lead everywhere, right away up to the top of an outstanding cliff where towers the castle-like 'gompa', to which Eliza Messaz and I climbed after we had pitched our tents, and drunk a cup of tea, while a crowd of Ladakhis stood around finding fun in watching us. Quite a few lamas and nuns were among them. Coming to the outer doors of the 'gompa' we were greeted in a friendly way by some lamas and invited inside. Though Lamayuru is a suitable place for a student of Lamaism and Buddhism, Thibetan history, language and customs, a Christian missionary may have the interest, but not the time for these things; similarly so with exploration, and the study of the birds, beasts and flowers of these little known parts of the world. It is the people who are his true interest, and his great concern is how to bring them to Christ. In the gompa we wanted to speak to the lamas of Christ, however unique the paintings, the idols and the buildings. The lamas who received us were those of the 'Red Hats', and not the more reformed 'Yellow Hats'. We found ourselves disappointed with them. They had apparently been drinking 'chang,' an intoxicant made from barley, and were actually drunk. Of no philosophic cast of mind, but very materialistic, they were spoiled by being near a main caravan trade route to Central Asia, and consequently to tourists and hunters. Neither missionary nor tourist is allowed there now, for it lies beyond the cease-fire line between North-West Pakistan and India. Though the lamas were apparently venal we had no wish to blame them overmuch. They have few comforts, and scarcely any luxuries. They lit burning brands and led us into one of the main chapels where they staggered about under the power of the drink brewed from the 'nas' or barley. They also took us down among the furtive shadows of the 'gompa' to an imposing row of figures of the Buddha, and halted in front of the main and central one which possibly was that of Bodhisat Chenrezig who is also manifested through the Dalai Lama under the form known as 'The All-Merciful Lord,' not so much a personality in himself but rather a stage in the Noble Eightfold Path. There are different forms of Buddhism. The Mahayana form of it in Thibet has been corrupted into Lamaism, the ancient religion of the country, a form of demon worship, and though this has been, as far as we know, destroyed by materialistic China, it is still practised in Ladakh where the Red Dragon cannot bite. It is too much under the power of India for that; and Russia is on its borders.

In the gloom of that inner hall of the lamasery we stood dwarfed by the figures in front of us, and regretfully conscious that we were not to have reasonable converse with the lamas. They pointed to a large bowl of rice set in front of the massive central figure, with coins stuck here and there in it, and, using a word for worship, invited us to add to them. We certainly would have given something, but the idea of worship attached to it we could not agree to, and we quietly told them so. We explained to them why we could not do as they wished, as we were Christians, and could not forswear ourselves before them. They were displeased, lowered their burning torches, our only means of light, put them out, and leaving us in darkness, withdrew themselves and told us we could find our own way out! This we did, stumbling and bumping along narrow passages until we found the low door by which we had entered. Soon they came tumbling out. Swaying in front of us, leering and grinning foolishly, they stood, and we spoke to them about sin, and the only Saviour, and left some Christian literature with them.

Bod Kharbu was our next encampment by way of the Futu La, (13,400), and the day following we moved on to Shergol near the source of the Wakha River which loses itself in the swift-flowing Suru, which in turn flows into the rushing waters of the mighty Indus at Olthing Thang. Before reaching Shergol we crossed the Namika La.

Another day's march brought us t oMulbeck Gompa, its walls gleaming white and fortress-like high up on the crags, a most amazing structure. The Ladakhi houses we passed were, in most cases, tastefully planned and strongly built in comparison with those of the Baltis. The people too looked stronger and better clad. We thought about their varied marriage laws, the Baltis and their polygamy, the Ladakhis with their polyandry, and how these laws affected them morally and economically. How attractively the lotus flower was carved on the stones of the prayer-walls, and the lettering of the heart cry of the Buddhist, 'Om Mani Padme Hum,' was beautifully inscribed with the flower. We passed and re-passed the fanciful 'chhortens,' those pinnacled repositories of the charred remains of the dead. But as messengers of the living hope, by the resurrection of the Lord Jesus Christ from the dead, our constant interest was the Ladakhis. Whenever possible we sought to make known to them this life-giving message.

On to Kargil and the fast racing Suru, more crossable there than anywhere we knew, though we failed in attempting it at one time. How refreshing the greenness around Kargil! The colourful bunched clusters of irises indicating boundaries of fields, is a bit of tasteful gardening indeed! Were permission granted, what a centre for further Asia evangelism Kargil could be! It is a focal point of so many races and various religions. Lamaistic Buddhists, Moslems, Hindus and Sikhs are all there, and it is one one of the main Central Asian Trade Routes. Thibetans, Ladakhis, Baltis, Kashmiris, Pakistanis, Indians and Turks jostle one another in its narrow passages.

In high Trans-Himalaya the dry air invigorated us as we pushed on to Tasgam, a pleasant place of many flowers, and on to Dras, a bigger place with a few trading shops, from which, moving on to ascend the Zoji La, we began to experience difficulties. Coming to a tributary of the Dras River we found the only bridge had disappeared. Deep and swift we could not cross it. It meant a toilsome journey for us all, far up our side of the stream until we reached its source, a great bank of snow in a deep cleft valley. Our next test was on coming to part of the trail which mounted high above a bend of the river. We found it had become so narrow that one had to edge along it, face towards the rock. To see if Jack Matthewson could manage over I crossed and re-crossed it. We knew then he could do it. Volunteering to retrace my steps, I took Makhmal, his horse, back down the valley, and led him over a crossable ridge, and brought him and myself to the party beyond the narrow ledge. In the climb Makhmal's saddle slid off his back and went down the hillside. Tethering the patient animal as best I could, I went down the steep slope, got the saddle on my own back and mounted up again. We both moved on in a world of our own. No one else was in it but the mountains and sky. I was glad when I could see the party. They were all across the ledge above the river. There was a shout and some cheery waving between us, and farther on we joined forces again.

We then knew that we might reach Matayan near Mitsahoi, with its ice and snow, that evening – our last stop before the Zoji La; but the Balti porters with Jawani and Phru Chik with our stores, and pots and pans, would not. We reached the wooden hut, at Matayan, as the heavy blanket of the Himalayan darkness fell. One man struggled through with a pan or two, and a quantity of rice which was kind and brave of him. Our dog, Bess, lay down where she had been running, when 'at one stride came the dark.' We heard her crying in the night, but could no nothing about it. All five of us lay on the wooden floor of the hut with a single blanket stretched across us. The cold air coming up through the seams of wood, made it a chilly experience. We could not go and call to Bess to join us for she might have tumbled into the roaring waters which were racing past the hut.

Our aim was to get across the Zoji La without delay to meet the two new missionaries, Ralph Moan and George Sach, beginning their ascent from the Kashmir side, to return with them to Baltal in Kashmir, and spend a day or so with them. Rex, Julie, Eliza and Jack were to go on to Srinagar for the wedding. The new workers were to cross the La to Kargil, in my company, on to Skardu, and to Doghoni It was a unique experience, the crossing and recrossing of the Zoji La in a matter of hours. The lowest of the Trans-Himalaya Passes it is not difficult of ascent or descent, but in parts it is a vulture-haunted carcase trail. Humans overtaken sometimes by storms or accidents suffer injury and death in the Pass.

After Scripture reading and prayer, in the first streaks of dawn we set off, led by a Balti guide, a man from the few poor dwellings at Matayan. Had it been broad daylight we would not have needed him; but there was a thin morning mist which would have made things dangerous for us. Following close behind him we had to keep the shadowy figure of our guide in view. One thought of the words of the Lord, 'I am the Way!' The guide that morning, and not the trail, was the way for us across the pass. We followed him. And what a reward! As we came down the Kashmir side, and began to see verdure and the first wind-torn trees below the snowline, there were Ralph and George coming up! After glad greetings with one another we all went down to set up our tents at alpine Baltal and have a day of heartwarming fellowship there. A fortnight's journey lay before us and unhappily both men had a touch of dysentery. They had acquired this weakening trouble somewhere *en route* on their eight days' journey from Bombay.

The hours of fellowship passed quickly, talking with one another, reading the Scriptures, praying and singing together. It was a delight to play the concertina that kind friends in Edinburgh had given Ralph to bring out to me. Next day George, Ralph and I set off up the steep slope towards the Pass. Every now and again we turned to wave to those below, until moving around a jagged rocky corner, we could see them no more. They would soon be wending their way through the lovely Sind Valley, Jack to go into the Mission Hospital in Srinagar for medical treatment, and then to go on home to Australia, where he had for a time been mourned as dead and a memorial service held for him. He got such a welcome on arriving that he said to the happy crowd awaiting him, 'Hi! I'm not the Governor!' Rex and Julie remained in Srinagar to prepare for their wedding at which I was to be best man. But there was to be many a march, crawl, slither and climb before that glad day.

We made good progress the first few days, and were moving on horseback across a broad patch of scree, with rivulets running here and there, when I was startled to hear screams for help. Since I was familiar with the terrain, I was leading, but hastily turned my pony's head around to see what was wrong. I was shocked and horrified at what I saw. Ralph had fallen off his mount. His feet had remained in the rope-loops which served as stirrups, and the pony had set off with fright at a quick gallop dragging him behind it. It was terrible to see and hear. George and I set off after him as quickly as our ponies would take us. We were relieved, before we came up to

The author (left) with
Jack Matthewson

The author (right) with Rex Bavington

Our Doghoni home

Doghoni Mission School—staff and pupils

Keeping fit at the Mission School

A Balti polo match

Phru Chik

*Pilgrims from Sinkiang on the
way to Mecca*

*A Balti
with goitre*

A Balti 'Zach', made of inflated skins

The author and Bess

Sarpha Ming and family

Balti homes

*The author crossing
Kharmang Rope Bridge*

Buddhists at worship

*A Kohat
Mosque*

Miss F. Davidson and friends in Kohat

Miss F. Davidson's home in Kohat City

Ron Davis

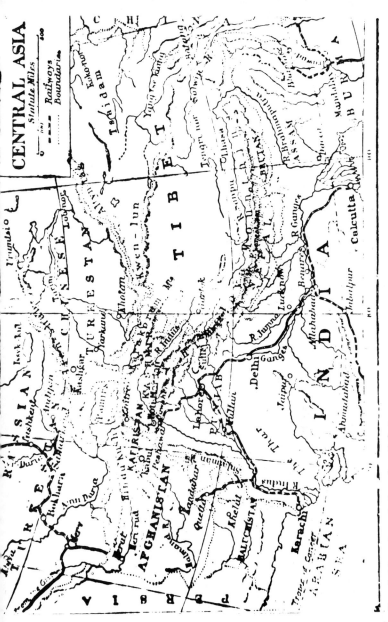

Central Asia as it was in the early 20th Century

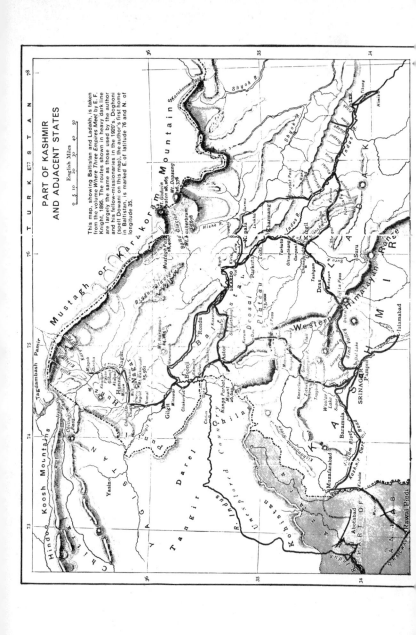

PART OF KASHMIR
AND ADJACENT STATES

English Miles

0 5 10   20   30   40   50

This map, showing Baltistan and Ladakh, is taken
from the volume *Where Three Empires Meet* by E. F.
Knight, 1895. The routes shown in heavy dark line
are largely the same as those used by the author
and his fellow-missionaries in the 1920's. Doghoni
(spelt Dowani on this map), the author's home
in Baltistan, is marked E. of latitude 76 and N. of
longitude 35.

him, to see his feet come loose from the rope-loops so that he was left lying among the rounded rocks while the pony set off on his own. Reaching him, and getting down beside him, we had time only to say a word to him before he fainted away. The worrying thought was that he might have fractured his skull in being crashed against stones as he was hurled across that rocky valley. When he came to we made a thorough examination of him, and were glad to find that he had no broken bones, though his bruises were many and severe. His head had been cushioned from serious injury by a large red plate-camera which he had carried hanging down to his waist from his shoulders. This had been wedged below the back of his head while he was being hauled along. What a mercy it was there! Before then I had chided Ralph about it, asking him why had brought such a clumsy thing to the Himalaya, where one should travel as lightly as possible. But the camera had saved his head, and possibly his life. We reminded ourselves, that, before we had set off that morning we had read of the preserving power of the Lord, in Psalm 121. It had proved true for Ralph, though now he was in pain all over, and could walk and climb but little. He sat on a horse for most of the journey while I walked by his side to see that he came to no harm. It was a very tiring and painful journey for him.

We carried six-feet-long sticks flatly tipped with steel. In various ways they were a help to us. They could be held out to help the person who had fallen into water or snow, and were useful for testing the depth and solidity of snows, especially where a snow bridge had formed over waters. To fall through one into the brackish swift flow can be an alarming experience. The sticks were a help, too, for keeping one balanced on rock ledges, and on narrow tree-trunk bridges, which presented little danger, although if one did fall, one might be carried by the stream to fiercer waters with no hope of rescue. Sometimes we crawled over boards, strongly underpinned, with drops of hundreds of feet below them.

At one point we came to a swift running stream foaming its way between rocky walls. A rather long and narrow tree trunk was laid across it. Not far away the Indus waters were crashing fearfully. We dared not think of what it would mean to be engulfed in them. Bess was with me. To my horror, she dashed on in front of me, sped across the tree bridge a certain distance, then began to wobble, and fell helplessly straight down into the swirling water below. Away she went, tossing and turning in it as it rushed towards the Indus. Divesting myself of my haversack and clothing, throwing aside pieces as I ran, I hurried along the rocky banks searching for a suitable place to enter the water to rescue the little dog, while the awsome boom of the great river grew menacingly louder. It is a fearsome sight, a Himalayan or Karakoram river rushing between its canyon walls. Swept this way and that way I could see that Bess was being carried farther from midstream to the other side. And, much to my delight, she was swept there. I picked up my few odds and ends of clothing, and was soon across the tree bridge, with Bess barking joyfully running towards me. How often I carried her across my shoulders when she tired; and helped her paw-pads with butter (mar), when they were cut and chapped!

On we went to Kargil, across Kharol Bridge, to Olthing Thang, Kuru, Skardu and Doghoni, and finally through the apricot trees to our much-loved home. Ralph and George were unwell and I stayed with them a week or two. It was strange, at times, to realise that we were in a land where no other Europeans lived. Great powers of nature were all around us. Not far away were the Masher-brum (25,678) and the Biafo Glacier. We did not know that the Shyock ice-barrier holding its vast lake of ice and water was again in a dangerous condition, and that the next year it would break, George would barely escape with his life and Ralph suffer much from exposure in trying to find him. The Shyock down which Rex and I had come from Khaplu on a raft of inflated goatskins would flood the valleys from mountain to mountain. The whole of Doghoni and its surrounding villages would be destroyed.

22: *K2 advance party encounter*

Ralph and George being fit enough to leave, I had been scaling rocks, wading through streams, and sleeping in the open. My footwear had been lost in the exertions. Entering Skardu I could see some very fine-looking green tents. They seemed Whymper ones, which only explorers possessed. Several Europeans were seated around a table, and were drinking tea. I went across to them. The tallest among them stood up to greet me. 'Hullo,' he said, 'have you been hunting bears?' I assured him that I had not, but that I was a hunter of men, a missionary. 'A mis-sionary!' he exclaimed. 'I did not know there were any missionaries in this country.' He was surprised when I told him that there were three of us, two of whom I had left some days ago, one recovering from an accident, and the other from sickness, and I had not found it easy to leave them. He said that he was the Duke of Spoletto, and he introduced the others to me, an Italian doctor, who was later killed in the Alps, and an admiral of the Italian Navy. The third man was a fellow-Britisher, the Sardar, or manager of their project which was the advance of the Spoletto Expedition, laying up stores to the edges of the glaciers below Mt. Godwin Austen in readiness for the full-scale attempt the next year. This expedition failed, but another Italian party succeeded a few years later.

The Duke asked me what I was going to do now, and what my plans were while I was in Skardu. I told him that for the present I would try to get a few vegetables, and make myself a kind of mixture known as 'tarkari,' which is Urdu for 'vegetable.' He would not hear of it and kindly invited me to eat with them, an invitation which I gladly accepted. Missionaries lived differently from explorers and hunters in the land of Baltistan, where nothing edible is wasted, not a crust of bread, or a leaf from a tree. All is gathered in for winter fodder for the cattle, and the withered leaves for fuel. The stones from the apricots are broken, the kernels eaten, and the shells used for burning. Mine were saved up in a sheepskin. And the Baltis have a system of field-latrines from which all refuse is used on their fields. By this means there is clean sanitation by comparison with some eastern lands.

As to my plans I told Spoletto that I was moving on to Shigar next day. This he was glad to hear, for their route lay through it, and I might be able to help them. While I was talking there, in that mosquito-less country, a hornet flew down the loose folds of my Balti smock and gave me a tingling hot sting. The doctor in his party gave it a touch of something out of the Expedition's store to ease it. Living as close to the people as we could, we had very little to come and go on by comparison. We were rather amused by the quantity of baggage, and the number of porters, that explorers and travellers were used to, while we had a haversack, our stock-in-trade, a few accessories such as some tea, when available, a jar with some sugar in it, and a few edible odds and ends. Life was hard for us most days.

That evening, at the meal, all five of us sat at a long table, the Italians on one side of the duke, and the British on the other. I enjoyed the conversation very much until the Sardar Sahib broke in with, 'Do you believe the Bible?' I said that I did. 'All of it?' he asked. 'Yes, all of it,' I said, 'Cover to cover.' His Highness kept on taking his soup. There was not a sign of 'for' or 'against' on his face. He said nothing. Said Sardar, 'You surely do not believe that Jonah was swallowed by a whale.' I affirmed that I did. 'Old wives' fables' said Sardar, 'Old wives' fables!' I felt affronted and ashamed. It had been a long time since I had seen any Britisher except my two fellow-missionaries, and now the next I had met was scoffing at the Holy Scriptures. He might have raised a smile at my expense, or even a laugh, but Spoletto remained inflexible. I admired his good manners. Being a Roman Catholic he kept addressing me as 'Father!' The other two spoke no English. I had an uneasy feeling that all was not well between Spoletto and my fellow-countryman.

Their beds were like the rest of their equipment. Just the job! It was dry and warm, and, as usual, I chose the most accommodating bit of ground available, where I read a few verses of Scripture, gathered a couple of blankets around me, and using my haversack for a pillow was soon fast asleep. I had no night clothes. Pyjamas wore out or were given away. Because of postal regulations for weight of mail being carried across the passes some of our mail had to be left for six months or more on the Kashmir side. It was a happy experience once to come there, and find a parcel of three suits of pyjamas sent to me by a very fine old lady who had come to Christ while a young girl in Glasgow, in the Moody and Sankey Campaign, and who lived to be over a hundred, being interested in missionary work till her call to Him whom she loved. These suits of pyjamas were greatly valued, and very useful to me, and to others, as they went their way down the line, in the Balti social strata!

It was, as ever, for me, to be off on an early start; but by the Duke's kindness I had breakfast with his party. They were moving on to Shigar, like myself, and I offered to help them in any way I could, and was soon on the job. Spoletto told me he would remain in Skardu. We walked along to a part of the River Shigar before its confluence with the Indus, but even there the flow was broad, fast and cold. It was our usual place of crossing. I knew it well. We chatted as we walked. He time and again addressed me as if I were a priest! There were crowds of Baltis, hired as porters standing on the steep rocky banks; and some Kashmiris too, and mountain ponies and piles of baggage and stores. My all was on my back! We were used to crossing on a 'zach,' the craft made of inflated sheep and goat-skins, but the Duke had acquired a good-sized, shallow-bottomed wooden boat. I could not see a nail in it. It was held together by adeptly used wooden wedges, and a type of wooden pin. Spoletto asked me to superintend the first load of humans, animals and stores going across, and so loading began. He stood on the rocks above, calling down one thing and another and seeing from his vantage point how the operation was going. I had a feeling of apprehension lest the 'nayo' (boat) should be overloaded and said so. The loading stopped. The polemen who knew the currents of the Shigar prepared to push us off from the lower rocks. The exploration party watched us from the crag above. Soon we were away, the first boatload of the advance party of the Spoletto expedition to Mt. Godwin Austen. I sat down quietly towards the front of the boat. The horses remained steady, but would have to be well watched as we moved into the cross currents of the river. The pilots knew them well and would guide us in their strong flow, though the crossing would take time, for we would be taken some distance down stream. We had no fears about the boatmen. They knew their job, but the craft was heavily loaded. The lash of water against it became rather rough, making it rock while the pole-men applied their poles vigorously. Cold spray hit us now and again. I looked at the gunnels of the boat. They were certainly low in the water. But we were moving on. I was not troubled. It was all part of life in Lesser Thibet. After all I was where the Master wanted me to be. Earth, river and sky were all His.

We were at about the roughest part of the crossing when a strong hand slipped into mine and held it firmly. It belonged to a young Kashmiri man sitting opposite. He spoke to me, saying, 'Look at the water! It is coming over the sides of the boat!' I nodded assent. He held my hand tightly. 'What will happen if this boat turns over?' I told him that the water was very deep and cold. It was coming from the glaciers towards which we were going, and if our craft capsized we would not have much hope of surviving. 'I am much afraid,' he said, 'and would like to hold your hand till we get to the other side. I see that you are not afraid.' I agreed, and told him to hold on, at the same time asking him if he knew why I was not afraid. He said it was because I was a very brave man! 'Not at all!' I said. 'Not at all!' I asked him if he had ever heard of the Lord Jesus Christ. He said he had not; though he may have done so after the Moslem fashion. Look up he would not. He kept looking down at the floor of the boat. 'Well,' I said to him, 'there is a sacred book called the New Testament, and it is part of the holy Book of the people called Christians, of whom I am one. It tells us about one named the Lord Jesus Christ who came from God and was sacrificed for us and our sins on the cross of Calvary. By knowing this and believing upon Him we have salvation, that is, we know our sins are all forgiven, and we have assurance of eternal life. And, not only that, but I am sitting here trusting in Him, and at peace from fear. It is this faith in the Lord Jesus Christ which I have which makes you think that I am a brave man. It is because I am trusting in the Lord Jesus Christ!' He said that he understood all I was saying and that it was all good; but he let go my hand as soon as we reached the shore, and kept well away from me. Onwards we went, the long straggling line of us, over the stretches of fine sand, and into the defiles and rocky paths towards Shigar.

Shigar became the base for the advance towards Askole and the Biafo Glacier, and thence to the Baltoro Glacier. Near my house in the Haramosh Range the green tents went up, and piles of baggage accumulated while scores of Balti porters gathered. Our Shigar folk were very interested. Piyara Dost and Jawani were amused at the grand commotion. But signs soon began to appear that many of the Baltis enrolled as porters by order of their superiors were unwilling carriers. Rebellion showed itself. Sardar Sahib had come but found it difficult to cope with the situation. Strikes took place, and not being conversant with the Balti Thibetan tongue Sardar came asking if I knew of anyone who could help. The very man for the job was there, Piyara. He took on the task of marshalling and instructing the Balti porters. Lines of them were soon moving towards the glacier regions, all working under their own leaders. I felt sorry for them. They were paid a mere pittance, and yet, in the case of many of them, money was of little use. They lived more by barter of goods. No wonder they rebelled at being called to such an arduous task!

The Duke of Spoletto remained in Skardu. Sardar Sahib and I were often together, sometimes in my home or out on walks. In our talks the main subject was religion. He got tired of it, and said to me, 'Purves, there is my tent. Come in with me and tell me what Christ has done for you. It may be if I judge you to be a sincere man in what you say, I might turn and yield to Him too.' We went into his tent, and he laced down its door-flaps so that no one could disturb us. We sat facing each other. 'Go ahead,' he said. 'I shall listen without interruption.'

I told the Sardar about my conversion to Christ while in my twenties, after a period of mental and spiritual confusion when I thought that I knew more, and better, than all I had been taught; and how I took to reading what atheists and agnostics had to say, such as Darwin, Spencer, Haeckel and Huxley, but that conviction of sin was ever with me although I did not know what it was at that time. Over and over again in my thoughts, words and actions, I was conscious of selfishness, inability and failure. Friends spoke with me, one in particular, telling me to become decisive for Christ. During most of my young life I had read the Scriptures, prayed, and attended worship. Now Scripture began to come alive to me, and the Lord Jesus Christ became a challenge to me; I understood in a fuller way than I had ever known that He had died for my salvation, and that the wisest and best thing for me to do was to trust in Him completely, yield to His claims, and give myself to Him without reserve. I did just that, and my life was wholly changed. All this and much more I told my friend, for by this time friend he had become. I went on to impress upon him what Christ had meant to me since I was born again; what He was to me as we sat and talked together; what He would be to me lifelong, and through all eternity. He sat silent. I said to him, 'Sardar, this is one of the most important moments of your life.' He said nothing. 'What about it?' I asked him. 'Are you coming to Christ?' He shook his head, 'No, Purves. I cannot,' he replied. 'Why?' I asked. 'Is it Jonah and the whale?' He smiled faintly. 'No, it's not Jonah and the whale. It is just that my life is full of entanglements. There are things in it I cannot tell my nearest and dearest. Back in civilisation there is so much to put right.' I tried to show him that the Saviour was able to clear it all up, to deal with the guilty past, to give him a clear and bright present, and the promise of a worthwhile future. 'Oh,' he said, 'you just do not know what you are talking about. It cannot be done.' I pleaded with him, showing him that if he would repent and come to Christ, God would order his steps, and would unravel the entanglements. But he would not have it. Things were so serious that nothing could be done. Explorer and missionary, there we sat in a tent, the Haramosh Karakoram all around us. God the Creator was not our theme, but God the Redeemer in Christ, and the soul of a man! He unlaced the tent door, and we stepped out into the brilliant summer sunshine. My spirits were low. It was not so-called intellectual difficulties that were keeping my friend from the kingdom of God, but 'a life full of entanglements,' a life in which there was so much to put right. Deeply conscious that a man at a time of his greatest need and opportunity had made a grave mistake, I crossed the polo-ground to my home to think, and to pray.

With the valuable help of Piyara Dost the big move towards Mt. Godwin Austen continued. I said farewell to Sardar Sahib, moved on south to Skardu and there met Spoletto who expressed disappointment when we spoke about the progress of the expedition. He showed impatience and displeasure when we spoke about his manager. Speaking rather sharply he asked me how he was getting on with his work in Shigar, adding that he thought the finance for the advance was being used up too quickly. I wanted to show him how awkward the situation was in Shigar and that Sardar Sahib was doing his best with people who did not care whether Mt. Godwin Austen was ever scaled or no. They could not care less. Why should they endanger their lives, far away from their wives and children, for the sake of the whim of some mad Europeans! All that they were getting, for doing so, was a few Indian rupees. The help of Piyara Dost was an asset, I told him, and every rupee given to him was profitably used. 'You will see that for yourself, sir, when you go up there.' He expressed a sense of displeasure in Sardar which I could not share. I feared for the man with whom I had become so friendly, and for his work. Before long I took farewell of the explorer, the Duke of Spoletto.

Later I heard that my friend's tenure of office had ended. Something had happened. There was a rumour that he had finally left the expedition hurriedly. Probably, all would have been different had he repented and trusted in the Saviour. As soon as I managed to get into touch with him in North India, we corresponded. I sympathised with him in the loss of his post, and challenged him again about his need of Christ, and the futility of life without Him, saying to him that he knew I was a satisfied man because of life in Christ. Wondering when we had parted in Shigar what I could give him as a token of

[103]

appreciation of his friendship I asked him if there was anything he had seen in my home he would like. There was. It was a little compact box, pocket size, of finger and toe, wound and burn dressings. Bought in London when funds were low I had felt there would be a use for it. I was pleased to give it to him. In reply to what I had written to him, he said he agreed with it all, but for himself nothing could be done, and he was not returning to Britain, but was going to Australia, there to breed and train racehorses; which seemed to me akin to a leap out of the frying pan into the fire.

H.R.H. the Duke of Spoletto returned the following year to the climbing of Mt. Godwin Austen, but failed to reach its summit. (It was not until a few years later that another European party succeeded in doing so.) He became engaged to be married to Princess Irene of Greece, sister of the Duchess of Kent, and in a letter said that he was grateful for the kind thoughts and good wishes from my wife and myself for his own and his future bride's happiness. Their years together were not many. I thought well of him and was very sorry to hear of his death.

23: Baltistan farewell

Having been requested by the Worldwide Evangelization Crusade to proceed to the North-West Frontier Province, a few Baltis and I set off on our fortnight's trek to Srinagar via the Burji La and Deosai Plateau hoping to reach them without much difficulty. But somehow or other, we missed our way and found ourselves at what appeared to be the source of the Salpura River. The wall of rock upward was sheer, shutting us off to the swell of water coming from a heavy fall from above which kept up a swift flow, broadening and deepening the river. We stood looking at it wondering what to do. There was no other way but to cross, and we had no craft of any kind available. A Balti kindly suggested that I might have his horse, and that he and his son would strip to the skin. He would go to the horse's head, and his son to the tail, while I sat astride the animal. With the others watching we got ready and entered the water. All went well at first but the river deepened and the rush of the current was strong and fast. The plucky little horse was being lifted bodily. The bed of the river was composed of stones rounded and bevelled by centuries of wear of water and provided little sure grip to the hooves of a horse, or the feet of a man. Then it happened! Away we all went in the whirling current. The hooves of our mountain horse were pounding about my head, fortunately without hitting it, as we all were swept over, and scrambled out on the other side. Finding what I thought was a secluded place I divested myself of all I had on. The sun was shining brightly and I laid out everything on the rocks to dry. But not so far away there were some Balti homes. I was conscious of eyes watching me from among the rocks and stony places! The others crossed putting their clothes on their heads and wrestling through the river.

The ability to swim was an asset. In Baltistan and Kashmir we were often 'in peril of waters.' My own most dangerous experience was in the usually calm and beautiful Dal Lake, Kashmir, where I might have lost my life as did one of our WEC missionaries, a few years later. Out on the lake I lost my bearings and control, and went down into the depths. A Kashmiri had taken me out in his boat and I had dived, and swam around it. Suddenly I became powerless and went down. Coming up I tried to grab the side of the boat but missed it, coming up I grabbed again, but it was the 'chatai,' the low hanging and sheltering straw-matting, I got hold of. With it, away I went again. I determined to make an all-out effort to grip the boat or get near to it. I was in grave danger. In God's mercy, coming up, I found myself close to the craft, and gripped the side of it fast. Hanging there for a few minutes, with the help of the boatman, I clambered into safety and lay there.

With our clothes now drier, we formed our group again and began to climb up to the Burji La. Again we had views of mountain grandeur beyond description, making me pray often that I might appreciate worshipfully what I saw. On scaling the La we started on our journey across the desolate Deosai. No storms hit us, but we had severe night frosts when the Baltis, as always, formed themselves into a human ball, unbelievably, in the open. In the cold clear air of the dawn I had to go and shake this frost-encrusted bundle, like a rounded beehive, to get it to break up. Piyara Dost's helpmeet had made me a number of small cakes to last me as bread for the journey, but she had enriched them too much with the familiar 'ghi' (clarified butter). They went bad. But, though I could not eat them, I held on to them, in case of need arising. I was in a land where to waste anything was a sin. In due time we descended from the Deosai and moved on to Minamarg (the green and fresh meadows). Central Asia was left behind. The air itself was different. It was now balmy and the tang was gone. How refreshing to be among trees, flowers, vegetation, pastures and cultivation! On to Gurais we went, where I stayed in one of the unique wooden huts of the Dard people, with the veteran missionary who lived among them during the summer months, Mr H. C. Robertson, a prayerful servant of the Lord. When he knew that I still had my cakes he humbly offered to buy them from me! I gave them to him with the warning that they might make him ill. He did not think so. He seemed to be more hardened to the missionary life than I was. What a pleasant expansive valley is that of Gurais, with a friendly people inhabiting it! It is thought by some that they may be of Grecian origin descended from the armies of Alexander the Great in his Asian campaigns. Strangely enough, the name 'Gurais' is pronounced almost like 'Greece'! With its log-huts dotted here and there, Gurais looked a miniature Swiss township; but I soon found that the huts were not as comfortable as they looked. It was good to know that the people there were being reached with the Gospel.

We were now in the deep cleft vales of the Kishenganga with forest-clad mountains all around. Soon we would move over high Himalaya ridges by way of the Rajdiangan Pass at 11,800 feet. Treeless itself, from it one can look down upon forest after forest of unbelievable green beauty. The Rajdiangan is exposed to freezing winds and heavy snows, but when we crossed it was a day of clear skies and bright sunshine. From there, I saw a marvellous and unforgettable sight, that of Nanga Parbat as I had never seen it before. What a spectacle of nature's grandeur! With all my experience of Himalaya and Karakoram, this peak reaching up into the ethereal blue, a resplendent white pinnacle of glistening beauty, with its supporting peaks magnificent in themselves, held me and raised my spirit up beyond and above them, making me marvel at their Creator and Upholder. There was the gracious realisation, too, both then and on other occasions, that there are times in life's journey when we see the Lord, and the glorious truths of His salvation, more clearly and more believingly. In seeing Nanga Parbat that day I saw a wonderful thing. There are more, far more, wonderful things to see in His law, and in His salvation.

I looked and looked again, and began moving forward, only to stop after the first few paces, turn around, and look for a time spellbound once more. On again, and again a turn around to gaze worshipfully on and upward to Him who, before the mountains were brought forth, was the Eternal. As I then moved forward on the Raidiangan Pass, which probably means 'The Pass of the Courtyard of the King,' in front of me I still saw and gazed with awe on Nanga Parbat the wonderful!

On we went, passing through Zitkus, and on to Tragbal, a region of unutterable beauty, where Rex Bavington maintained he once saw the Three Bears! At any rate he saw 'Father Bear, Mother Bear and Baby Bear,' come out of the forest, frolic for a time, and go back again into the woods. I saw little of the wilder animals. Certainly never a 'Hyeti' (Yeti) which I think is a kind of bear. One day Rex left me while the snow was falling in Doghoni and encountered a snow leopard. For a time he maintained it was a tiger! We were new to the land then! And then again he met another! But he parted on very good terms with both. His most trying experience was when, on horseback, somewhere between Skardu and Shigar, he was chased by wolves. But I had few wild animals experiences. I did have an experience about the use of a gun when I wanted to use it for food by trying to shoot one or two of our blue wild pigeons. We often, because of lack in the country, suffered as did the people, and were pleased when they sold or gave us a wild blue pigeon. That day on which I went out with the firearm I climbed

steep rocky slopes, lay, and hid behind rocks, fearful in
their barrenness, and used up a great deal of energy and
time until the Lord spoke in my heart telling me that my
energy and time were His, and that I had been sent to the
Baltis to tell them of Him, and that I was to keep separat-
ed to the Word of God and prayer, and He would pro-
vide my table in that wilderness, which He did according
to my need, and so the gun stood in a corner, never to be
used again.

From Tragbal one could drink in the beauty of the
Vale of Kashmir with its wooded mountains, the winding
Jhelum, carrying the waters of a thousand streams, the
Wular and Dal Lakes, and Bandipura township which
we must reach before we could journey across the Wular
to Srinagar, the City of the Sun, on the farther side. In
Bandipura, I stayed in the empty mission-house, and was
amused to see by the light of my hurricane oil-lamp that
fleas were jumping high from the dust of the floor! But I
was glad that there were no house-bugs about the place.
What with the fleas and a play of some sort going on in
the moonlight not far from the mission-house with some
obscenities in it, and musical instruments playing, it was
not a restful night. My Baltis found a place in the
caravanserai.

The Baltis and myself were all foreigners now. Strange
bobbed-hair men from the Karakoram! Next morning
we hired a Kashmiri boatman and his 'dunga' to take us
across the Wular Lake to Srinagar where in due time I
met Rex and Julie Bavington! 'So you have turned up,'
Rex said. 'Yes,' I replied. 'When is the wedding?' He
looked with a smile at me. 'Wedding,' he said, 'we have
been married a fortnight! You are very late in coming!'
It was certainly very late for the best man to arrive. But
then it was after months of arduous travelling. And now

we were asked to proceed to the North-West Frontier Province, the Bavingtons to Peshawar, and myself to Kohat, and to have as colleagues there devoted independent workers, Miss Flora Davidson, Miss Maria Rasmussen, and Mr Donald Fullerton.

24: *A seeker after truth*

Srinagar is an interesting place. There is, for instance, the Masjid Hasrat Bal (Mosque of the Prophet's Hair) where at selected times and seasons a phial is brought out with a single hair in it said to be from Muhammad's beard! When it is shown to the assembled worhippers, the pushing, rushing and crushing are incredible! Enthusiasm extraordinary! Not far away is the hill called the Takht-i-Suliman (Throne of Solomon). The eminence has a Moslem name, but there is a Hindu temple at the top of it, linqam-shaped stones helping to adorn it. Gaily-dressed pilgrims climb up to it to worship. Quite close by, at the bottom of the hill there is a narrow road which, for part of its way cuts through an old Moslem cemetery, and one can see, in either bank of it, cavities exposing places of interment with the remains still visible. Though the defile was not long it had its sombre message and one day I was unexpectedly startled in it. A man was walking at some distance in front of me, and suddenly he left the centre of the road, went over to one of the grave openings in the bank, picked up what appeared to be a leg-bone, or an arm-bone and went on in front of me whistling a tune on it! I could hardly believe my eyes and ears! It shook me! I did not catch up on him, and he managed to evade me. Making enquiries about the incident I was told that there was a joker who sometimes waited about the passage, deposited his whistle on the edge of an interment cavity, and when some unwary person came along he picked it out, pretended that it was a human bone, and marched on in front playing a tune on it!

Another day near the Takht-i-Suliman when crickets were chirruping merrily, and the aroma of sawn-up deodar and chenar trees was around us, a young man, intelligent looking, and evidently well educated, came and said that he wished to speak seriously with me about religion. As we sat down together he told me that his surname was Pande. I was interested in the name. It was held in respect among Hindu people. Restless, and apparently troubled, he said that he had not long before been with Sadhu Sundar Singh at Sabathu in the Simla Hills, but that he was now living with Moslem friends, seeking spiritual truth and fellowship, but finding none; and he added tersely, with scathing words, that while there existed a Koran there would exist a hell, meaning that such was necessary for Islamic people. It sounded harsh but I knew that I was in the company of a disgruntled and distressed young man troubled about his salvation.

Quietly he advised me not to be in a hurry to 'make' him a Christian! 'Think well of every word you say. Consider well if you yourself believe what you ask me to believe. It may cost me much. I had a brother who became a Christian, and he was poisoned, and died. Talk to me seriously, but do not hurry me.' These were some of his expressions and they were truly realistic.

We talked for some time, but finished very much as we

had begun. I urged upon him the just claims of the Lord Jesus Christ and faithfully told him what the Holy Scriptures said about Him, about man, about S. P. Pande himself, about sin and salvation, the necessity of repentance and of faith. It all finalised in his saying that he could not make any definite decision as the cost might be very great, but that he would go 'into the "jangal" to battle it out alone'. 'Jangal' in Urdu, means a forest or wood. There are many of them in Kashmir.

There was another meeting and another parting. Before he left me he brought out a book saying that he would like me to have it as a reminder of the occasion. It had been given to him by its author, Sadhu Sundar Singh. 'Take it,' he said, 'and by it remember me. It is an expression of appreciation of our time together today.' After prayer he went away, and I wondered if we would ever meet again. We never did. The book he gave me was a copy in English of a work, first written in Urdu by the Sadhu, 'Reality and Religion, Meditations on God, Man, and Nature'. It was inscribed, 'With kindest regards to bro. S. P. Pande from the author, Subathu', which would seem to indicate that Pande must have shown Sadhu Sundar Singh evident interest in the Christian faith. It had been a personal copy of the Sadhu, for it has a date in it with his signature sometime before the date on which he gave it to Pande. But the underlinings and notes in it are those of the latter. At one point where Sundar Singh writes, 'Who else can heal the broken heart except Him who is the Creator of the heart,' there is a marginal word, saying, 'True,' and this is followed by a note about his being deserted by some friends 'just after the death of my beloved brother.' His forenames with their initials S.P. I never got to know.

For some who have never lived in a non-Christian or

anti-Christian community and environment, such as an Islamic or Hinduistic one, it may be difficult to understand what it means to be a faithful servant of Christ, or a faithful convert to Christ. One has to be loving, wise and kind, but also faithful, if possible without rashness, and it is just here that an inner struggle might ensue, as, for instance, in Shigar, Baltistan, where we had written and painted a beautiful display text for the Mission House door – 'I am the door: by me if any man enter in, he shall be saved, and shall go in and out and find pasture.' (John 10.9). When it came to putting it up, I had an inner battle which brought me to my knees, in prayer, for divine help. Why? Because someone might read and believe, and in such an environment as we were in, all the powers of evil which Satan could bring against him and us would be let loose. It went up! We know of no one being arrested by its message, but it was a word of the Good Shepherd where wandering sheep have not heard his voice and call.

25: In a frontier fort

Some two hundred miles west of Srinagar, Kashmir, is Kohat, in what was the North-West Frontier Province, and is now North-West Pakistan. Donald Fullerton and I wanted to reside in Kohat City and evangelise from there. For permission to do so we went to the Superintendent of Police for the area, a kindly Scot, Major W. D. Slesser, who could not suppress a broad smile when we made our request. 'Well,' he said, 'they may not cut off your heads the first night, but I would not be sure about the second.'

We managed to smile. He was against our proceeding any further with such an idea, and said that he would not help us, even if he could. Permission from a higher authority was necessary. We went forward with this, but were told that residence in Kohat was not possible. Rooms near the Mia Khel Gate were offered. We took them for a time. Free access was granted at any time into the city.

Slesser Sahib moved away from Kohat to take charge of the Pathan Police Force at Shabkhabar Fort. I used to see him there, and mingle to some extent with the men of the Force, in the hope of influencing them for Christ. I went with them to sham-fights, to the rifle range, even out to look for raiders. It was interesting to be with Slesser Sahib when he was judging cases brought before him. A fair-minded man, conscientious and prayerful, he certainly was an asset to the people he served. A good horseman, Slesser Sahib had been a polo player, and he was keen for me to go into the riding school with the cavalry recruits. I got used to the commands of the instructor, 'Stand! Walk! Trot! Canter! Gallop!' Accustomed as I was to the ponies on the Thibetan uplands, it was another matter to be mounted on a cavalry charger!

One day, watching a training session, I saw that the Pathan instructor had a mettlesome steed. I was glad that I was not on its back. A fine mount was given me when I was called into the ring. 'Stand! Walk! Trot! Canter! Gallop!' All went on splendidly. Slesser Sahib was watching every move. To my surprise he called to me to exchange horses with the instructor. Doing so, I wondered what would happen. Away we went at the word of command. How I would get on I did not know, but I thought I knew how I would get off! The Major, and others of the Police Cavalry, were standing on the other side of the wall. Sensing that my horse knew that it did not have the instructor on its back I imagined that I might soon join them there! Up he went in front! Up he went at the back! He drove forward! He backed! Again upon his forelegs! Down again on his backlegs! He was a good horse with an unskilled horseman. The training stopped, and he was relieved of his missionary tyro!

Another of his stable gave me a gallop. When quite a distance from the fort he decided to make for home. He knew he was carrying an amateur and not a tough Pathan horseman. We flew like the wind. John Gilpin-like I clung around his neck as we sped on to the main entrance of the fort, which for defensive purposes had a blank wall facing us as we entered. A sharp left or right turn would take us into the parade square. Now for it, I thought! He would smash right into the wall. But not so. Quick as a flash he veered left and on into the middle of the square. There he stood. I got off his back. He looked at me know-ingly as if to say, 'That's how I do it. That's how it is done. Do you want to go out again?' I said, 'Yes, I do!' Mounting him, we trotted out through the gate, and down the road that we should not be seen on after sun-set, or we might be seen again in a sadder setting. He was wonderful, and treated me as if I knew something about horses. We came home in dignified cavalry fashion.

An Indian doctor was resident in the fort, and that evening he said to me, 'I think that you should give some money to charity.' Asking him why, I received the reply, 'I watched you galloping to the fort without any let-up whatsoever, and expected you to crash against the baffle wall. I shut my eyes. When I opened them you were on the parade ground.'

Not far off the road were the graves of nineteen British troopers. Mohmand tribesmen had been on the rampage, looting and killing. These soldliers were sent to stop them, and if possible, take some of them prisoner. The raiders crossed a stream and lay hidden among tall, thick sugar canes. On came the troopers, and halted at the deep stream. It was fatal. A hail of bullets mowed down men and horses in a horrible heap. Cruel knives were then used upon the wounded. None escaped. In the evening Mohmand women came and mutilated the bodies. Night by night, till daylight came, it was reassuring to hear the watchmen cry in the town below the walls of the fort, 'Khabardar! Khabardar! Take care! Take care!' It told us that, as far as they knew, all was well.

But Slesser Sahib and I knew that, 'Unless the Lord keep the city the watchman waketh but in vain.' Our trust was not in any one or in anything but the Lord. We had our times of Bible reading and prayer, and when he lay in his hammock, during his siesta, I used to read to him choice portions from the Word of God. While I pulled the 'pankha' (large fan), we talked about the Lord and His ways with us. His interest deepened in the Holy Scriptures. He had learned them in his boyhood and his youth, and now, by faith, they came to life in him. The time came when we had to part; and neither of us liked that. As we talked things over he said to me, 'I can let you go. I now know what it is to be born again.' He was a servant, a servant of his country, and a servant of the peoples of the Afghan Frontier.

26: Bibles in blankets

Donald Fullerton was an ex-officer of the United States army and a gracious and able soldier of Christ. No words of mine can express his worth. Together we read the Holy Scriptures and prayed, tended each other and evangelised. Our time with one another was all too short. He went from me to worthwhile work among students and Jewish work at Princeton University. For years he was President of the Princeton Evangelical Fellowship, and was honoured by a doctorate of divinity at Princeton. He was the helper of all who were interested in Christian missionary work.

Comparatively speaking, we were not far from Quetta, scene of tragic earthquake disasters, and were not surprised one night when a severe tremor shook us out of our sleep. We hurried outside to see our world askew, and enveloped in an eerie windless silence broken only by the terrified howls of pariah dogs. It was a sweet relief when things came straight again, enabling us to go on with our everyday work among the people, often praying about our being allowed into Afghanistan, particularly Kabul.

No missionary, as such, at that time, was permitted to enter Afghanistan. Applying to get in as tourists for a stated period, Miss Flora Davidson and I were refused entrance since we were British. The applications of Miss Maria Rasmussen and Donald Fullerton were granted, the one being a Dane and the other an American. They were allowed a month's stay in the land. Donald and I felt that it was a bad law that kept copies of the Holy Scriptures from going into the country. We decided that when he and Maria Rasmussen went in, quite a number of parts of the New Testament should go with him. We had to plan how it should be done. Like true Eastern travellers they had to have their bedrolls with them, and we purposed that Donald's blankets should be lined with Scripture portions. They were laid out on the floor, and neat rows of Scriptures enclosed in them, a few copies of the New Testament among them. They were in Arabic, Pashto, Persian, Urdu, and English. Rolling up the blankets we put them into his bed-bag. Lifting it, to feel the weight of it, I laughed till the tears were rolling down my cheeks. The weight of the bed-roll was that of three! Quietly, he sat, looking at me. 'Why the merriment?', he asked. 'Why the merriment? Simply this, when you come to the first Afghani Customs Post and the officers lift your bed-bag, they will say that it is the heaviest one that ever was in the world.' He looked serious. I felt so too. 'Then what?', he asked. Again I had a fit of laughing, and I assured him that he might be sent back to me, or lodged in an Afghan jail, or maybe shot. There they were. He tried lifting the bag, and ruefully admitted that it was a heavy roll of blankets! The Khyber Pass and Afghanistan on the morrow, and a man intended to break the record for heavy bedding going into Kabul!

We waited on the Lord that night, and assurance was given to us that the Scriptures could be taken into Kabul, and all would be well. Others things had to be settled. Together we diligently prayed, planned and talked, and became sure of what we were doing. A code of writing was devised for our correspondence with each other, since we knew that our letters would be censored, so that while the things we wrote were quite true, they also had another meaning; for instance, I could say that the flowers around our doors were growing beautifully. This could also mean that the believers were growing spiritually. He was to write appreciatively of the land and its people, something that every missionary should do. If called to serve a people with the Gospel, one should never vilify them when among them, nor when speaking about them in one's own country. A piece of paper was left with me by Donald saying that if he was not able to return I was to use the moneys and things he had not been able to take with him.

Next morning, he and I and Miss Rasmussen, with their baggage, boarded a crowded char-a-banc for Peshawar. Passengers were all over it. They were in beside the driver, on the running boards, and on the roof with their stringed bedsteads. As the 'chara' climbed up the Kohat Pass it was a solemnising sight to look over the cliff sides and see the remains of buses, lorries and cars lying far below. Their passengers had all been laid away with the inevitable Muslim word, 'It is the will of Allah!'

The ribbon of road we were on went through Yaghistan (Tribal Territory), and only one road was under the authority of the government of India. Passengers could get off the bus, dash down into a trench which led to their fort-like home and maybe receive a spatter of bullets as they did so, the missiles coming from another fort-like house not far away. A Pathan to whom I spoke about this cruel blood-feuding said that I should not speak to him about this for we had the same thing among the Scottish clans; There was a gun-making factory not far off this road, and I had an unpleasant time one day in its vicinity among tribesmen fondling gun barrels, locks and butts. Their last word was an invitation to see over the factory the next time I was around. One did not go to such places sight-seeing. It was only when the path of the

Lord's ordering went that way. It was laughable when there was any blocking of that narrow road. The driver, where it was possible, simply took his vehicle through the hedges, made a detour through the fields and back on to the road again! All things considered we often returned uplifted from such journeys!

Arriving in Peshawar I went with Maria and Donald to the driver and car which had been hired to take them up the Khyber Pass, over the border, and on to Kabul. Waving them farewell I then went into Peshawar city to spend a short time with my Worldwide Evangelization colleagues, Rex and Julie Bavington, before returning to Kohat, and to report to Flora Davidson.

Maria and Donald got to Kabul, and a very few undetailed letters passed between us. Rebellion had broken out there, and leading men had been assassinated. The country was in a ferment. No further word came from our fellow-missionaries, and we wrote no more to them. Weeks passed after their month of stay. We continued in prayer. Then came a happy surprise. One day, Donald arrived at my door, saying as he came in, 'Let me in quickly, and lock the door. I think that all the newspaper reporters in India are after me!' I did not see any! Whatever his experience of them while coming up country, no reporter came near us. We soon were drinking tea together, and talked and talked. I had not yet seen Maria Rasmussen. She had gone up home to her colleague, Flora Davidson.

Donald told me his interesting story. He said that once they were over the border, the car they had hired began to give trouble. It went on and stopped! Went on and stopped! And stopped! They were miles from Kabul. It was almost dusk. They sat by the dusty roadside and prayed. When it seemed that they might have to sit the night through in the darkness, a man with a horsedrawn two-wheeled gig (tonga), came along. He stopped and asked them if they were stranded. They said that they were, and that they wanted to get to Kabul. He offered, at a price, to take them there. This offer they gladly accepted. Bundling their belongings and bedrolls into the vehicle away they went, and arrived in Kabul. They realised that they had not been brought into the city by the usual way, nor had they passed through any customs or guard-posts at all. The Scriptures in the blankets had been safely preserved. 'And,' said Donald, 'we got every portion and New Testament into the hands of responsible readers.'

Their latter weeks in Kabul were a trial to them. Riot and rebellion! Shootings and deaths! They tried to get out of the country, but could not. The way to the Khyber was closed. An Afghan agreed to take them by car out of the land via Ghazni and Kandahar to Quetta. It was a long and hazardous journey with grave dangers. They were chased by brigands who shot at them. When they had left them behind the car-driver would persist in going to his Muslim prayers, and threatened to leave them to their fate. The robbers, on horseback, would appear again. Away they went again! In the deep sands they had to use strips of carpets to keep the wheels going. At a rocky bend the car ran into a line of camels, knocking down the front one. Immediately the leading camel driver lifted his rifle to his shoulder and aimed it at the car-driver. The world seemed to stand still! Donald endeavoured to take a photograph, but was stopped by the cries of Miss Rasmussen who feared for their lives. From all that he told me there was no doubt that they had had a severe experience, and Donald felt that his time in these parts was over. He advised me also to move.

Having been in the midst of the rebellion he felt that it might reach where we were. Being an independent worker Donald could leave an area whenever he wanted to do so. I did not think that the Afghan troubles would come across the border to us, and besides that, being in a missionary fellowship I would have liked to confer before moving. One of the Afghan leaders did come to Kohat at that time, made some speeches, and got back again to Kabul only to be assassinated.

27: Daniyal a brother

One of the few Pathans in our area to be converted to Christ from Islam was given the name of Daniyal, which was slightly flattering, perhaps, and yet not altogether so, for there were traits in his character which made him worthy of the name. He dared to stand alone and to show openly that he belonged to Christ and would not bow to any other. For this he had to suffer. Possibly the missionaries expected too much of him in leaving him in charge of some saleable Christian literature, and some rupees. When they returned from the hills Daniyal had gone with both money and books. It was probably a mistake to leave him like that, with no other Christian Pathan that we knew of in the city of Kohat at that time.

I was displeased, and did what I could to get into touch with him. It was a very mean action, I would tell him. My attitude towards him was unreasonably hard. Acquiring an address where he was said to be I wrote letters to him telling him what I felt. I got the odious length of saying that what he had taken was 'God's money,' and he must return it. My conduct was shameful, showing lamentable ignorance of his heritage and circumstances. After all he was a Pathan reduced to poverty because of his Christian witness.

Came the time when I set off for his country village where I had heard his brother lived. Meeting him was no pleasure. It was a dark experience. Greetings over, I asked him about his brother Daniyal and whether he had any news of him, since I had lost all trace of him. Looking intently at me he quietly and firmly said, 'I have no brother.' Thinking that he had misunderstood my enquiry, and my intentions, I again put my question to him. Again he gave me the same answer. We stood looking at each other. I ventured to make clear to him that I was a friend of his brother who had become a follower of Christ and was now known by the name of Daniyal. If he knew where he was would he please tell me. Coldly he said to me, 'For the last time, Sahib, and I hope you will understand this time. I have no brother!' I understood, and nodded my head in assent. No brother! He had said what Daniyal could say of both him and me, 'I have no brother!' No brother! Having expressed wishes for peace for each other I made my way out of the village, matching the paltry price of a few books with that of being a Christian Pathan. Over and over again the words rung within me, 'I have no brother.' Appalled and ashamed at my unspiritual attitude I confessed my sin to the Lord. Poor Daniyal, I thought, no brother in the flesh, and no brother in the Spirit! I determined to look for him with something of the eagerness of a shepherd and the welcoming love of a father.

Through bits of news, and circumstances, Daniyal got to know that we would be glad to welcome him back again. And it happened! One day while I was working in the small garden patch near the 'hujra' (guest-room) of the lady missionaries' house, I saw him coming! Downing my tools I ran to meet him and threw my arms around him asking him to forgive me. I was forgiven. He was forgiven. The joy of it all that happy day!

We were building our place of worship on a slope near the Mia Khel Gate which closed at dusk, and Daniyal, unashamed of Christ, worked with us. Sometimes he did not look well, and one day he told me that he was losing strength. Not long after this, while he and I were talking together near the unfinished building, to my deep distress he had a severe haemorrhage from the lungs, and became seriously ill. There was no adequate medical provision for him. I offered to nurse him in my own small home. To this the lady missionaries would not agree, feeling that it was unwise to do so. The building went on, but Daniyal built no more. He stayed in the home of some kindly Pathan friends, preparing for 'a house not built with hands, eternal in the heavens,' and in due time was received there by the Master of the house.

28: In the Khyber hills

There were times when we felt like packing our bags to leave the North-West Frontier Province. A dream, at a time of testing, helped me to stay. It was easily interpreted. In it a Pathan tribesman challenged me to a duel. I hesitated. We stood facing each other. 'Wakhlah!'

'Take!' I said. It was a grim encounter, but I won. I woke up. I had to stay.

One of my difficulties was that I had been used to kindly Baltis, cheerful Ladakhis, and peaceful Kashmiris. Now, to be with men who could be fair to my face, but whose hands were stained with blood, tested my friendship with them. I could not get used to arriving at a home and being ordered away from it because someone had just been shot, or to seeing weaker individuals badly treated by the stronger, like a Chinese trader whom I had to rescue from a group who were roughly handling him. Stranger from afar, he gave me a linen table napkin for my trouble. To be where black flags flew was not a comfortable experience. They meant wounds and death. One day coming upon a grim warrior sitting near his ominous sable pennons the usual greetings just did not fit – 'May you never be tired!' and 'May you never be poor!' He was going somewhere! A handsome enough man he was, and armed to the teeth which were strong and white. A few rolling r's and gutterals of Pashto were soon exchanged between us, and he told me he was ready for a fight. The sight of his rifle and knives appalled me. I suggested to him that surely he was not going to maim and kill people. Condescendingly he smiled and said that this was exactly what he intended to do. An Indian was there, 'Yes,' he said, 'and he will kill you too!' This was rather a startling idea. I managed to raise the semblance of a smile to my Pathan friend. 'You surely would not do a thing like that,' I said to him. He shook his head. 'Not at all,' he said. 'Not at all.' Fear was not much of a trouble to me on the Afghan Frontier; but at times a sickening horror would come over me, for murder is a most terrible and awful sin against God and man.

There was also the battle between minds renewed with

the light of life in Christ Jesus, and minds blinded by powers of darkness. In this war one was apt to get spiritual and mental wounds which drove one to the Great Physician for healing. In the work of encountering the minds of Moslems, Hindus and Buddhists, we had valuable experience of spiritual warfare. To challenge them to faith in the Lord Jesus Christ and the Gospel was to meet with an unbelieving antagonism, and often, sarcastic blasphemy, that shocked us. Missionaries can be wounded spiritually, mentally, nervously and physically, and may come out of such encounters with thought processes, attitudes and manners of speech they never imagined they could acquire. I had a colleague who was wholly dedicated to the evangelism of Moslems in Central Asia, and when we were back in Britain and sitting together in a missionary committee, as he took part in the discussion, I could hear the hard tones of Islam as both of us had known it. It sounded out of place, crude, and ungracious. Sensing this himself, he said to me, 'I am speaking like a Moslem mullah! How strange! I shall tell you first what I wish to say and you can say it for me.' It was evidence of his dedication to Moslem evangelization and of the unexpected possibilities of prolonged involvement ministering among the unbelieving and hard of heart.

There were varied reactions to the people of the North West Frontier Province among our visitors. Some were interested in them while others did not like them at all. The Pathans made anyone take a measure of himself. We missionaries often did so, and got used to it. I smiled one day when I took an ex-army officer friend up the full stretch of the Khyber where our constant meeting with tribesmen worried him. The more he met these tall, and well-armed men, with faces like those of ancient Greeks, the more nervous he became. At length he said to me, 'Do you see this bulge in my pocket?' He tapped a solid thing. I said that I did, and hoped, in myself, that no tribesman had seen it. 'Do you know what it is?' he asked. Of course, I knew. 'It is a revolver,' I said. He nodded, saying, 'I am at such a pitch that, if one of these chaps comes near me, I think I shall shoot.' That would never have done. It would have been the end of us. 'Do you have one with you, Jock?' Assuring him that I had not, and would never have one, I told him that to be without firearms was a defence, for if the people of these regions knew that I carried such a thing, they might do me hurt to obtain it. Being a Christian himself he understood me when I said that by day and night the Lord was my Defence.

A football match in the Khyber was quite different from one in Baltistan. As evangelists, whenever there was a lawful way of coming closer to the people we took that way, so, when Rex and I were asked to go to Jamrud in the Khyber, and play for a British army team from Peshawar, we agreed to go. The opposing team was one of athletic Pathans who played in their bare feet as we ourselves often did. They had hearty support too. Around the field stood many others of the same martial race. A number were armed and I hoped that some of them were police!

The game had not long started before we knew that it would be a tough one. As centre forward I was in the thick of it and sometimes was thudded to the hard ground of the Khyber. There was a pleasure in getting my breath back, looking around at the smiling spectators, getting up to their applause, and joining the fray once more. It was a rough but happy encounter in blazing sunshine. Several of our side were showing wear and tear as I was myself with a bit of a leg knock. There was rather a comical experience too. A Pathan player left the field and a substitute came on for him. He plunged into the game with all the usual zest of his race, and soon he and I were in a tussle. His enthusiasm was unbounded. He managed to get on to my back and I wondered whether it was soccer or rugby he was playing! I was relieved when he came down again.

We changed clothes in a long wooden hut and were doing so when there was a knock at the door. Someone went and returned saying that a Pathan was there who wished to speak to the 'sahib' who was involved in the funny incident towards the end of the football match. My colleagues looked rather wistfully at me as I rose and went to the door. A pleasant surprise awaited me. A smiling Pathan was there. Greeting me warmly he said, 'Sahib, I have come to bring our apology to you for how you were treated towards the close of the football match. The lad who jumped on you has never played at football before! Please excuse him for his foolish antics. I told him that I thought it was absolutely splendid of them to think of such a thing as this kindly apology and explanation. I appreciated it greatly, and asked him to convey my very friendly greetings to the eager young footballer. That was a cheering experience in the Khyber. There was a sad incident next day. Two British officers were shot dead by tribesmen not far from Jamrud.

What had playing football, with Pathans, to do with Christian missionary work? My answer to that is that it was part of the general pattern of life from day to day, as we tried to keep close to our fellow humans for the Gospel's sake, where one had to prove oneself a man in what was very much a man's world.

29: Had he heart faith?

In Islam there is a belief in a general resurrection and a
final judgment with rewards and punishments of
sensuous interpretation. We never tired of telling people
about the Lord Jesus, the Resurrection and the Life. We
were alert whenever we heard of anyone who might appear to be convicted of sin, and was stretching out his
hands if haply he might find Him who gives life from
the dead. I heard of a leading man in Kohat whose
generosity of character and deeds was much appreciated,
and it was said that he had an interest in the Christian
faith. Thinking that he might be one whose heart the
Lord had touched I went to see him and had a talk with
him. It was a disappointing visit. He was a firm Moslem
and apparently self-righteous. No one ever sent for us,
asking, 'What must I do to be saved?' The thousands
around us did not know, as Samuel Rutherford wrote,
that 'Grace alone is the garland on the heads of the glori-
fied.' We did not forget it, and any appreciative word
spoken by a Moslem for the Saviour was like a gleam of
sunshine to us, and inspired us with hope that we might
meet someone whose heart the Lord had touched.

One day on entering a village and meeting its leading
man I was enthusiastically greeted in English with, 'Welcome! Welcome! I am glad to see you,' and a big smiling
man shook me warmly by the hand and invited me to sit
down on the string-bed (charpai) beside him. We were
soon engaged in conversation about Christ and Muhammad, Christianity and Islam. At one point he looked
brightly at me and said, 'It may surprise you to know that

I have been in Australia!' It did! 'Yes,' he said, 'I lived there at one time and I met one of your kind there. He tried hard to make me a Christian.' This was interesting. 'Oh,' I said, 'What did he say to you?' He laughed heartily. 'Say to me? Say to me? He said a lot to me, but I forget everything except one thing.' When I asked him to tell me what that one thing was he laughed merrily. 'And you really would like to know that one thing he said to me that I have not forgotten?' I said that I would, and off he went with a smile into the unforgettable part of the story of the Australian who spoke with him about Christ. It was most interesting.

Said the Australian, 'If you were on your way, Mr Pathan, to a greatly desired haven to which you had to go and to which you had never been before, and you came to crossroads where there were no signposts of any kind to give you directions, you would come to a halt, no doubt, considering which was the right road to take, and the more so if there was nobody about from whom you might enquire. What would you do? What could you do? A road went this way, another went that way, and others went other ways, and a well-worn path was close by. How important to take the right road. Halted! Puzzled! Troubled! Ah, but who are these over there on the bank by the roadside? Two men! One, by the look of him is evidently sound asleep. The other is wide awake! Which one, Mr Pathan, would you ask to show you the way?' At this my burly Pathan friend burst into uproarious laughter, and slapped his great limbs in merriment. Up he jumped. 'He had me,' he cried. 'He had me!' The meaning was crystal clear. 'Yes,' I said, 'he had you.' He jumped around in delightful excitement, crying over and over, 'He had me! He had me!' and slapping his thighs in happy glee. Then he stood quietly looking at me quizzically and kindly. 'And what was your answer?' I asked. In mischievous merriment, he bent over to me and said, 'I said to the Australian that I would go and shake the sleeping one and ask him!' I shook my head. 'No! No!' I said. 'You would ask the one who is ever wide-awake, the Lord Jesus Christ, risen from the dead, and alive forever more!' We sat and talked together about the mysteries of life and death, sin and salvation, earth and heaven. I thought well of our Australian friend. It was such a happy visit. All visits in Pathan villages were not so. I thought we experienced that day something of the joy of Christ's resurrection morning.

30: A chauffeur in Kabul

I tried, lawfully, to obtain entrance into Kabul, but without success. Often I stood at the stretched-out barrier pole at Landi Kotal at the end of the Khyber looking into Afghanistan, but dared not go any farther. From the hillside rocks machine guns manned by Ghurkas pointed at us on the British side, and armed Afghan sentries paced it out on the other. Not a yard farther was permitted. Crossing over meant being arrested and handed over to the British who would probably have sent me home. This would have been a setback for missionary work since prohibitions would have been put on other workers. There was the possibility that one might have been shot first and questions asked afterwards. I applied to the British Deputy Commissioner for permission to go to Kabul for a short time, and he told me that I could go if I had a personal invitation from the British Ambassador-in-residence there. I did not get that. I did not feel it was right, considering all of the circumstances involved in asking for it. But I did apply to the British authorities for permission to reside and work nearer to the Afghan border. To that request I received a sheet of foolscap. On it were a few words all built up into an emphatic refusal.

But there was Yu'hanna', a national, brought up by Mr and Mrs Andrew Paterson, and living not far from Kohat. It was good news when we heard that he was to take a post as a chauffeur at one of the Embassies in Kabul. Yu'hanna' was a Christian. We were glad that he would be a witness for Christ in that needy city, but our rejoicing was mixed with trembling. We had the alternate beats of the missionary heart, beats of faith and fear. We did not hear of him for a while. Then the painful news reached us that he had been attacked and severely injured.

In due time Yu'hanna' (John) returned to the Frontier and came to see me. What a pleasure! Out together for a walk and a cup of tea he laughed as he stood by watching a wayside barber shave me with an open razor and without soap, Indian-style. We got into a corner of a 'chaekhana' (tea-room) and the hot steaming 'chae' was soon brought to us. So as not to attract attention we gazed around the walls at the brightly coloured pictures of British troops being routed by Afghans, and listened to Afghani melodies being played on some stringed instruments. In a hushed voice he told me how his car had been stopped by a group of Kabulis who dragged him from it on to the road, held him there, took out the battery from his car, and poured the acid from it across his throat. His tongue, gums and throat were badly burned, and he suffered much. He showed me his mouth. Parts of his gums were not there at all. It was evident that he was severely tested by the ordeal. 'You cannot go back to Kabul, Yu'hanna', I said to him. 'You cannot go back.' He smiled. 'Oh, yes,' he said, 'I can go back. I am going back. There in Kabul I shall help to represent the Lord Jesus.' He returned there. I never saw him again. There were rumours of something serious having happened to him, about which I was never clear. A Sikh sent out a message from him, given in his last hours. 'Tell the missionaries that I died a Christian'. It is a hard thing to be hated unto death for the sake of Christ.

31: *An outcaste not cast out*

Brightly intelligent, he was fluent in English, but could neither read nor write, and preferred to be known as Bhai James or Brother James rather than by any other name. Of low caste, he was amongst the crowd of those who came to our meeting on a Saturday night. It went on from about ten o'clock and finished at almost midnight, and was held for those who said that they could not come to a service earlier in the evening because of work, and for others who could not come to worship on Sundays. It was a 'Prem Sabha' (Friendship Meeting), and was held in the open in our 'mahalla' (sweeper quarter) where our first place of worship was. This, in time, became my home and Christian families lived around me. Carpets were laid out for rows of folk to sit on. Hand drums thrummed out their beat in rhythmic unison. Hands clapped joyfully, one's own, and then one's own with those of one's neighbour. Psalms sounded out into the night, with their

[133]

lovely North Indian melodies. Scriptures were read, and thanksgiving to God for the Lord Jesus Christ. Moon and stars shone brightly down on us as we together enjoyed our 'jalebi' (sweetmeats), and gallons of 'chae' steamed their way among us. An idea was born! Someone proposed that one of our number should come along to me during the week, learn some words of Scripture and repeat them aloud to the gathering at the next Prem Sabha. Bhai James was their first choice.

James came along during the week and I felt that a few words from 'the glorious sixth of John' would be suitable and settled on the last few words of verse 37 – 'and him that cometh to me I will in no wise cast out,' prayerfully hoping that they would find a niche in the heart of the learner, and in the hearts of those who would listen to him at the Friendship Meeting. Sitting down we repeated them over and over again, in English and in Urdu, these words of the saving welcome, 'and him that cometh to me I will in no wise cast out;' but it was in Urdu that Bhai James took his final stand, 'aur jo koi mere pas aega, use main hargiz na nikalunga.' He repeated it; I repeated it; together we repeated it, 'and him that cometh to me I will in no wise cast out.' Then something wonderful happened. A quietness fell over us. We stopped speaking. Bhai James looked at me wonderingly. It seemed as if Someone else was with us. Someone else was saying the words. In a whisper James asked me, 'What is the real meaning of these words? Of whom do they speak?' I told him that the words were spoken by the Lord Jesus Christ about Himself and His saving grace and power for all who come to Him. In the stillness around us I asked him if he had ever really and truly come to Christ, and if not, would he come now? He told me that he had never really come to the Saviour, 'but I will come now,' he said. And he came.

We rejoiced together in God our Saviour. His cup of salvation ran over with the gladness of sins forgiven, and joy, the fruit of the Spirit of God, was in full bloom with its branches spreading over the wall. Eagerly I told him how John Bunyan came to Christ relying on these very words, and how he was so filled with the joy of his salvation he felt he could have preached to the crows sitting on the ploughed lands before him. Bhai James was one for whom there was no place in the castes of Hinduism. An outcaste from them he was an 'outcast' who was welcome to Christ.

Visiting him in the small and humble home where he lived with his young daughter was a delightful experience. I could stand in the middle of his living-room floor and by stretching out one's arms almost touch the walls of the room. He would say to me, 'Now, before you say anything, or read and pray in this my home, let us both stand together, and let us say together the words that are the most wonderful words in the world to me, "Aur jo koi mere pas aega, use main hargiz na nikalunga."' And this we did while his wide-eyed child looked and listened.

The Prem Sabha came and went, and the time came when I, also, had to go. Again there was the singing, the talking, the fellowship, and the cups of tea. Bhai James and our mutual friends would make me a gift, much as I had appealed to them not to do so. Their choice of the gift was also a thing from which I tried to turn them, but all to no avail. Some of them went into Kohat bazaar, bought a piece of gold, and had it fashioned into a ring for me. Kohat is inscribed on it. These simple hearts in the early stages of Christian living wanted me to have it as a visible seal of a fellowship between us. As such it was given and received.

32: Missionary and mullah

One of the mullahs in Kohat had one eye, and this made
me feel sorry for him. All the same, he did not like me at
all, and when we happened to pass each other in the
street I could hear him muttering to himself, 'Shaitan!
Shaitan!' Whether he was thinking of me as a demon,
that I was on the devil's work, or that he was invoking a
curse of the devil on me, I just did not know. Sometimes
we actually came face to face in the bazaar. One day,
seeing me up on the open platform of a shop he rushed
up the steps to stand beside me. His attitude said, 'Now
I've got you!' With a voice that all could hear, and barbed
with sarcasm, he shouted, 'How many "mater log" (outcaste people) have you now made Christians?' And he
thrust his face into mine, giving a fearsome growl. I felt
that not only he but everyone who heard the question
should hear the answer. Squaring my shoulders I called
out loudly and clearly, 'Many! Many! Oh, many!' He
leered at me in scorn. However much we had been told
about the inadvisability of preaching forthrightly that
the Lord Jesus is 'the only begotten Son of God,' I felt that
I could not take any more of such rudeness to the Gospel.
Lifting myself up so that everyone in the crowd could see
me as well as hear me, I slowly and loudly, and with
emphasis, quoted John 3:16 in Urdu, and the mullah
being nearest heard best of all! The wonderful message
finished in a silence in which everyone seemed to be
turned to stone. All were looking intently at me. No-one
spoke or moved, and I quietly walked away.

Quite unexpectedly we met another day, I out with a

haversack of Holy Scriptures to sell, in various languages, Arabic, Urdu, Hindi, Gurmukhi and Persian. Some would buy them to read secretly, others to destroy them, and some would buy them out of friendliness. In the vicinity of one of the main mosques a strong hand gripped me, from behind, by the coat-collar, and the gutteral voice of a Pathan said, 'You are coming with me.' 'Coming' was not the right word to use, but I certainly was going! The Pathan saw to that. Up through a long passage he pushed me, and on into a large room where a group of men were sitting. In the midst of them was Ankh Ek, or 'One Eye,' the mullah. About two dozen were seated smoking hookahs. A few weapons were lying about. My usher dumped me down beside the mullah.

Evidently they had seen me close by, though I was unaware of them, and had sent out my captor to collar me. Assuming the role of chairman, he said to the mullah and me, 'Now we want you two to talk, the one for our Prophet Muhammad. Peace be upon him! The other for the Prophet Jesus Christ.' All chorused, 'Certainly! Certainly!' I looked around them. They were big strong chaps, all of them, and Moslems to a man. Knives and guns were beside them. Our district was a dangerously cruel one. Some of the weapons used were ghastly things, such as a cane walking stick, the handle of which was a small sharp axe-head. It was reckoned there were two murders in the district every three days.

'Well,' I said, 'seeing you have me here I'll gladly speak to you about the Lord Jesus Christ, provided I am allowed to speak about Him as He should be spoken about, and without you grasping your knives as I speak. What is the point of me talking at all if I am not permitted to say what I believe to be the truth? Give me your word of honour that I will be allowed to speak about the Lord

Jesus according to the Scriptures, and without you injuring me, and I shall speak, telling you who He is, what He has done, what He is doing, and yet will do.' Their deeply resonant voices chorused agreement.

They listened with apparent interest while I told them of Jesus the Christ, the Saviour of the world. I was enabled to show them quietly and clearly, according to the Christian Scriptures, his virgin birth, his sinless life, his atoning death, his triumphant rising from the dead, his ascension up to heaven, his coming again for His people, and to judge the secrets of men, and that the evidence of the Holy Scriptures shows him to be the only begotten Son of God. There was not a murmur. Even Ankh Ek listened and never said a word. He was asked to speak, but would not do so. Why, he did not explain, but the group seemed to understand why. The Pathan who had rather roughly brought me in, now very politely and smilingly asked me to get up, and he would show me out. Along the passage we went into the brilliant sunshine. I was a little amused, but grateful, when he showed me the shortest and best way to reach home.

It was an interesting life to be in and out, day and night, of Kohat City, where Europeans were allowed in only a matter of yards, unless accompanied by someone responsible, or by armed sepoy guards. An airman said to me, 'It's amazing that you go about in that city at all times. I have often flown over it but have only been a few yards inside its gates. Some day I would like you to take me into it.' We had no meeting-place inside the town, but there was the mission-house built by Miss Flora Davidson, who, with her colleague, Miss Maria Rasmussen, bravely lived and worked there. And there were some humble people belonging to the Lord who also lived within its walls.

33: Old soldier and quack doctor

Ramzan was a big, burly Turki, who maintained that he was a Christian but whom we never had at our Fellowship; living away up among the distant hills he was isolated from us. We heard that he acted there as a 'hakim', a quack doctor. We just did not know what to make of him, as far as his faith was concerned. He was nice enough to know, and yet it was a relief to us that he was a considerable distance up the valleys, and did not get us into any difficulties with his cures. And then it happened!

I had taken to sleeping under a mosquito net on a camp bed near the door of the house. The sun had risen that morning with burning heat and was blazing down, although it was only about half-past five, when a seemingly monster figure stood by my bedside calling, 'Sahib! Sahib! Are you there? Sahib! Sahib!' I lifted up the mosquito net. It was Ramzan, all the muscular six feet of him, with a cheery smile all over his big round Turki face. 'Hullo, Ramzan, what are you doing here at this time of the morning?' He had someone else with him, a rather crestfallen old man. 'Oh,' said Ramzan, 'I have brought one of your own people to you, for you to help.' Getting out of bed was easy. Because of the heat, even sheets at night were a burden. The old Britisher gave me a nod and a smile, and I could see by his manner that he had 'gone native'. 'No money, no job, no anything,' said Ramzan. What to do? The old man was an ex-soldier who had decided never to return home. He had gone completely Indian, and where Ramzan had fallen in with him

I never discovered. Ramzan's plan was good, yet not so good. I was to take care of him! I agreed to do what I could for him, but the 'purana sipahi,' or old soldier, would have none of it. He made it clear to us that the days were gone when he was at ease living among his own people. He wanted to go on farther with Ramzan. With relief I agreed to this, and the two of them set off in the brilliant sunshine for the rocky home of Ramzan, among the Afghan Border hills. I felt very sorry for the old soldier. He gave me the impression that he thought he was still in India. Far from it! He was in Pakhtunistan, the land of the Pathans, 'where the bullet whistling down the pass whistles clear, "all flesh is grass."' In spiritual things he was apparently in the dark.

Several weeks passed and he turned up again, without Ramzan. He was in a very agitated and distressed condition. 'I've run away! I've run away!' he said. 'I could stay no longer in Ramzan's country. Help me to get back to India. Oh, what a wild land this is! Violence, violence everywhere!' His experience had been severe, and his nerves were shattered. Wanting to get away from the Frontier Province he appealed to me, saying that he had no money to go to India. I invited him to stay with me till he was able to go there. He would not hear of it, but said that he would go and live in Kohat Bazaar. Go and live in Kohat Bazaar! I had never known of any European doing that. I tried to show him that he could not, telling him that the city gates closed at dusk, and that no one was allowed in or out without a pass until the next day, and that even by day a European was allowed in only a few yards; though I could go in both by day and night. The lady missionaries were resident there, but I knew that he would not stay in their home if he would not stay with me. In vain I explained to him that there were the same bad people inside the gates of Kohat, as he had already met with at Ramzan's; that they would rob him of all he had, injure him, and probably kill him. The old soldier would not listen. Though he thought he was now a national of the country, India, I told him that he was not now in India, but among an Afghan people, very different from all he had been used to. He was deaf to all advice just as he was to any words about the Christian faith. Away he went through the gates saying all would be well.

Next day he came to me in a pathetic condition, nervously ill in the extreme. He had spent a terrible night. Those he had been with had mocked him, baited him, and beaten him. He was at his wits' end, and was now ready to run anywhere; he said that he could not live there another night. He agreed to stay a day and a night with me, which he did. Poor old sepoy! He was blind to the claims of Jesus Christ, as were those around us.

Talking together he told me about his time with Ramzan. It had such a comic side to it all that I could hardly stop laughing as the old man, so excited, told me of how that plausible quack doctor had passed him off to his people as a very famous American doctor! Ramzan had the common open-air platform for his surgery, with the usual twisted metal chairs and small tables. Steps led up to the covered platform where sat the beaming Ramzan and the old soldier now a Professor of Medicine! 'I sat in front of his shop all day,' said my old soldier friend. 'You see he taught me to tell the people to put out their tongues, to let me feel their pulse, to breathe in and breathe out, until I was sick and dizzy with looking at tongues, and feeling pulses.' Ramzan then prescribed Soda Mints, Gregory's Mixture, Castor Oil or something akin, for these sick, ignorant patients, while his supposedly learned colleague said a few meaningless words to him in English. It was a money-making contract in which the assistant doctor got very little. 'I thought I would go mad,' he said. 'The repees flowed in to Ramzan. But I've run away! I've run away! I am no great American doctor. I am only a poor old British soldier. What shall I do? What shall I do?' It was a most important question. Ramzan by this time was, no doubt, facing the music, and it would not be harmonious. I hoped that the 'hakim,' for his own sake would be equal to the occasion, and that none of his ungrateful patients would come our way. The old man was greatly shocked. He had seen something of how our Frontier people lived, their troubles, cruelties, blows and wounds, and was appalled. At his urgent request I agreed to get him away to India as soon as possible. He had no money. I had very little, but I determined to get him some. Next day I went to see an army sergeant, and asked him if he could explain the condition of the old military man to the men of the sergeants' mess, and ask them to contribute together to his financial help. He agreed, and I was able to give the old soldier more than enough to get him to India. After prayer with him I took him to Kohat Railway Station, and waved him away to Rawalpindi and more peaceful living.

34: Things which are not

We knew when Abdul Khadir was on his way towards us before we saw him. Deformed from birth, he wore wooden blocks on his hands, and crawled his way in a tortuous wriggle along the ground dragging his limbs behind him. Up through childhood, boyhood and young manhood he had come, from a respectable family. He was intelligent and well-educated, but physically he was a pathetic figure, and might have been tempted to say to God, 'Why did you make me thus?' A rebel against his Maker he could have become. But the Man of Calvary, the suffering Saviour, whose sorrow was like no other sorrow, had made his appeal to Abdul Khadir. Had he complaints of his state of being they were stilled. He could sustain no argument with Christ Jesus of the thorn-crowned head, the spear riven side, and the nail-torn hands and feet. For such as he are written these lines.

> 'Tis life indeed to live since Thou for me hast died,
> Thy human face all human filth rank stained – a guide
> To human heart. Above, all royal crowns to greet
> Pained nature's cursed bounty tied;
> Religion-murdered hands and feet,
> And soldier-torn Thy manly side.

There was a music in the clip-clop of his hand-clogs as he came towards us. Soon he was giving his cheery greeting of 'May you never be tired.' What a word, and wish, from such as he! One looked down upon the upturned eager face and returned the greeting with the fervent wish, 'And may you never be poor.' I hoped that he would never be poor except poor in spirit, which he truly was. They are rich that are so, 'for theirs is the kingdom of heaven.'

A great day came for him. The event was a debate in the Reading-room at Mansehra where red-haired and red-bearded Andrew Paterson and his wife faithfully served their Master. Moslems delight in theological debates, and we took them on when it was possible. Their Pathan tempers were sometimes rather short, and this did not help. That day our own speaker was Abdul Khadir. He would speak for Christ and the Christian faith. Who was to speak for Muhammad and Islam we did not know. Mullahs used to come into the Reading-room and talk to Andrew Paterson who knew his Bible well. Quotations from it were apt to silence them. One of them said to Andrew, 'Stop quoting from that Book. When you do, I have nothing to say. Please say, "I think", or, "I have come to this conclusion," or, "What do you think?" or, "Maybe this is the truth," and so on, and then we shall be able to talk and argue with you.' Andrew ever kept true to the Book and made full evangelistic use of it.

When the big day arrived, Andrew and I were there with our champion, Abdul, beside a table in the centre of the Reading-room. He was on the floor near our feet. In due time we would lift him up on to the table from where he would speak. Hemmed in by Pathans on every side there was hardly room to move. The place was crowded to the doors. The Muslim speaker arrived, courteous, sure of himself, a fine strong specimen of manhood. All the more so in comparison with the contorted form of Abdul. Scriptures passed livingly through one's mind such as, 'I who in presence am base among you,' and 'God hath chosen . . . the foolish things . . . weak things . . . base things . . . things which are despised . . . things which are not . . . that no flesh should glory in His presence.'

All was set in order. The hubbub ceased. Chairman and referees were ready. Our strong and willing arms were also ready. Andrew and I bent down and lifted Abdul up on to the table. His Pathan face, so Jewish in appearance, was alert and eager beneath the turban so neatly set around his head. He looked what he was, a Saiyed. One could feel there was a respect for him among the gathered crowd. What a picture for a painter! I admired him much, this brave witness for Christ among his own people, his only allies foreigners from another land. He assumed a kind of half-sitting posture, and in one of his hands he held a few notes. He was to me that day, and always will be, like a living personality from the book about Islamic converts to Christ, 'Sweet First Fruits,' or as it is in Arabic, 'Bakoorah Shahiya,' and in Urdu, 'Asmani Shirin,' or 'Heavenly Sweetness.' How one prayerfully wishes that Moslems would read that book in their own languages; and that Christians would read it in theirs.

The debate began. Abdul was elected to speak first. Raising himself up, as far as his awkward limbs would allow him to, he began. There was only one voice. It was his. Clear, firm and pleasing, all could hear him. Every eye was on him. His arguments were all related to the revelation of God in Christ, the world's only Saviour. Interest deepened and became intense. I looked around. The tall tribesmen stood in a square short-line phalanx, every face intent, every ear attuned to every syllable, and one could sense esteem rising for the twisted form upon the table, as if they were feeling that, though they did not agree with him, he was one of their kith and kin. How pleasant it was to know he was safe! I rejoiced within, and knew that Adrew did too, at the thought that no harm would come to the man upon the table, whose mortal

frame cried out for the day when all things will be made
new, this man who carried the wounds of Calvary in his
heart, crucified with Christ. He finished. There was a
murmur of voices; some consultation. It was intimated
that the debate was over. The mullah had listened with
interest, but he did not wish to speak. Reasons were not
given. We were quite satisfied. We had not won a debate,
but Abdul had comported himself as a faithful witness
for the Lord Jesus. And wonder of wonders, everything
had taken place in such a friendly manner. In the circumstances we could not have wished for more.

We all came out into the bright sunlight. The audience
moved away in twos and threes, while we spoke with
Abdul, encouraging him in the Lord. Wishing us peace
he crawled away with our wishes of peace upon him, the
sound of his hand-clogs telling us of his humble mortal
frame with the excellency of the power of God in it, that
power working in him which would mean, in the fulness
of God's purposes for him, his tortured body being 'fashioned like unto Christ's glorious body.'

35: Power for the faint

A smartly dressed young man met me close to the barbed
wire entanglements surrounding the city wall, and said
that he wished to speak with me. I politely nodded assent.
He said, 'It tells about our Prophet Muhammad in your
sacred writings, does it not?' I told him that as far as I
knew there was nothing written in the Bible about him.
He maintained that there was, and that actually Jesus

Christ had spoken about him, and that if I had a New Testament with me he could show me where this was written. I told him that I knew the words he was referring to, but they were not about Muhammad. 'Very well,' he said, 'let me see them.' The only New Testament I had with me was in English, and a British Army one at that. Taking it out of my pocket we turned to John 14 : 16, and I read the words to him, 'And I will pray the Father and he shall give you another Comforter, that he may abide with you for ever.' He came in triumphantly. 'That's Muhammad,' he cried. 'That's Muhammad!' Waiting a second or two I requested him to listen to the first few words in the next verse, and I quoted them, in Urdu, to him, 'Ya'ni sachchai ka Ruh,' and explained that they referred to the Holy Spirit, 'the Spirit of truth.' He retorted, rather annoyed, 'You have put that in yourselves.' Urging him to think honestly I tried to show him how unreasonable it was of him to imagine that I would have left home to come to such a dangerous place as we were in, if I knew that what I taught was a fake.

By this time the inevitable crowd had gathered, and we were hemmed in. Unfortunately my New Testament contained pictures of life in Palestine – of a man sowing seed, a woman winnowing corn, a shepherd and his sheep, and so on. My enquirer roughly pulled it out of my hands. The crowd was getting bigger, and pressing in on us. 'Aha,' he cried, 'you have pictures in it. Come and see, everybody!' He held it aloft for all to see. They chorused his delight. The fun had begun. For them! Smiling and winking to one another the crowd waited. I was to answer a few questions about myself and the pictures. The young man led them in the mock questionnaire. 'Why are you not dressed like this man?' The picture was that of a shepherd. Explaining why, I knew that

[147]

I was at a disadvantage, and had no-one to support me; but I had an audience to make the most of in a witness for Christ. Great surprise! 'You do not dress like this man in the picture! You have him in your sacred book! Why have you got this picture here? As I tried to explain why more questions came hurling at me from various directions. The show was on. The crowd loved it. Up went the New Testament for all to see, the pictures the focal point. 'And why have you not a beard like your man in the book?' I had to explain. 'Then why have you got him in your book?' So it went on. They laughed uproariously at what was, to them, an every-word victory. Young and old gathered for the fun. In unison they kept shouting aloud, 'There is no God but Allah, and Muhammad is his prophet.' Receiving my New Testament back, I felt that it would be unwise to take it out again among such folk, and had no sooner put it in my pocket, when a big burly Pathan, evidently a man of some consequence, pulling people away in front of him, came bouncing into the ring to face me. Up came a mighty fist swinging before me to stop about an inch from my nose!

This fierce new entrant into the arena told me what he thought of me, of my spying plans and purposes for the British Government, of the Christian faith and of Islam. I managed to keep breathing steadily while his fists swung menacingly. The crowd was absolutely thrilled. Time and again the Qualima rose loud and clear, 'There is no God but Allah and Muhammad is his prophet.' But finally he quietened somewhat, his threatening hands stopped swinging, and to the rousing cheers of the crowd he went away. He had won the day. I knew differently. There is no defeat in Christ. A fellow-missionary once said to me when a Moslem crowd pulled his violin out of his hands, and stopped us from singing the praises of the Lord,

'There are times when we have to appear to be defeated if we would have the victory!' Calvary tells us so. It too had every appearance of defeat.

Still there was the young man who had set things going. He seemed somewhat abashed. The crowd, now quiet, were there too. They listened to me for a little while and I told them that controversy was not enough, nor the apparent winning in it. I spoke to them about the love of God, that God was love, and love was of God, and that their need of knowing the love of God in Christ Jesus had been certainly apparent that day, by the way they had treated me. No one said yea or nay, and we all drifted away with an apparent sense of non-affinity with one another, except that we were fellow-humans, in need of love for God and man.

Reaching home, rather jaded, I was glad to sit down. Mosquitoes and sandflies buzzed around. A long centipede came out of a hole in a wall, ran across the floor and disappeared into a crevice. Lizards darted about, small cold-blooded things. I often found them in my pockets. Scorpions would soon begin their crablike antics. Of hornet stings I had had quite a taste, but I kept myself scorpion wise and had none of theirs. As I sat, my little friend arrived, a sparrow which had taken a fancy to roost on a ledge of wood, night by night. I like the Urdu name for a sparrow. It is 'chiriya,' and pronounced 'cheer-ee-ya.' I liked it especially that night.

As I sat, my jadedness became a waiting on the Lord, and I told Him that I was finding it difficult to be a messenger of the Gospel, and that I wondered how I could go on with these controversies where emotions and passions were so strongly aroused that they completely did away with reasoning and consideration for one another. Tired and tried, in my whole being, I sat slumped in the chair, when mildly and easily I became like a child listening to a kind and loving father, and I saw that I had been sent by him, the Father, to the Afghan Frontier to love the people, to have no desire to win debates or controversies with them, but to minister Christ to them in all of my thought, feeling, word, deed and manner of life among them. What ease pervaded my being. I knew afresh that I was learning of Him and finding His yoke easy and His burden light. His word to me was being graciously fulfilled, 'I will give you rest'.

36: Ahmed keeps his vow

His face suffused with joy, he came towards me with arms outstretched and saying so kindly and so happily, 'May you never be tired! May you never be tired!' Soon his hands were clasped in mine. I had never seen him before, and did not know who he was. An elderly Pathan, he reminded me of a fortress falling into ruin. In early manhood he must have been a fine figure. It was a brave thing for him to do, his coming right into the low-caste 'mahalla,' where I was living. Clad in the drab dust-coloured clothes that were worn by many of the Pathans, he had evidently travelled from afar. I asked him who he was. He said that his name was Ahmed Ghul, and he had come to talk. I invited him in and soon we were chatting together, and drinking tea. Not having room for him to stay with me, I felt sure that Miss Davidson and Miss Rasmussen would give him a welcome, and if their 'hujra,' or guest-room, was vacant would gladly have him to stay there for a time, as was indeed the case.

Later, when I asked him why he had come to see me, he related an interesting experience as the reason for his coming. He had got into serious trouble with his tribe, and it became evident to him that he was in grave danger of severe judgment from them. Terrified he cried to God to help him, vowing that if he did he would give him his heart and his life. 'That night of the vow,' he said, 'I had a dream. In the dream a man in white came and stood by me and told me that my prayer and vow had been heard, and that on the morrow my troubles would begin to vanish. And so it was; they vanished altogether. That man in white was the Lord Jesus Christ about whom you teach. I have come to fulfil my vow, to give him my heart and life, and be received into your Christian fellowship.' Hardly able to take in what I was hearing I sat silent. But an Indian friend was with us, and he spoke up saying, 'Oh no, Ahmed Ghul, that was not the Lord Jesus Christ who came to you in your dream. That was one of your own Muslim holy men.' The old Pathan shook his head with negative emphasis. 'No,' he said, 'that was not a Muslim 'pir' who came to me in my dream. It was the Lord Jesus Christ about whom the Sahib teaches, and I am becoming a Christian according to my vow.'

Our Indian friend started in from another angle. 'Do you know, Ahmed Ghul, what happened to the last Pathan who became a Christian?' The old man was all interest. 'No,' he said, 'What happened to him?' It was painful to listen, while the well-meaning individual told Ahmed Ghul how his fellow-Pathan had had his head cut off. Ahmed jumped up, and bowed before us, drawing his right hand across his feet, and saying, 'Though they cut off my feet,' and then drawing both hands across his knees, 'and cut off my legs,' and drawing his hands across his middle, 'and cut my body in two, when my spirit shall be with God who gave it, I am a believer in the Lord Jesus Christ, and I shall keep my vow.' My admiration for Ahmed Ghul was unbounded. But what a challenge to a missionary of Christ among a fierce Moslem people! In my own heart I made a vow that I would go through with him, no matter what the cost.

Together we enjoyed reading the Scriptures and praying. My Urdu Bible was a large one with very big print. As we sat at a table I read portions of it to him, about the love of God in Christ Jesus, of sin and salvation, of death and life, time and eternity, of God and man, and of God and Ahmed Ghul. He heard things he had never heard before, and was amazed at it all. Time and again he would lift the Book and clasp it to his breast while the tears ran down his weatherbeaten brown cheeks. Expressions of his delight in the Lord were like a perfection of praise. 'Oh, Sahib, Sahib,' he told me, 'how often, how often, have I been in this city, and never bothered to look your way. Now you are the only one whose company I desire.'

Days passed, and soon must come the time when he was to confess Christ in open testimony and be received into the fellowship. There was no doubt about it, he trusted in and loved the Saviour and was determined to pay his vow of full dedication to Him. He talked much with the lady-missionaries, and with me, and came to all the services for prayer and worship. So far not a dog barked against him. But one evening there was a break in our peace and quietness at a weekly prayer-meeting which I was leading. The door opened and a young man came in. I knew him well, and had often found him difficult to deal with. He sat down, but never spoke. Ahmed Ghul was there, and I could see that the lady-

missionaries were a bit apprehensive, and they signalled
to me to say nothing about the old Pathan. But someone,
Faquira, I think, the low-caste cloth merchant, began to
praise God for what He had done for Ahmed Ghul. The
difficulties had begun; the ladies were distressed; I wondered what the outcome would be.

The Kohati stayed all through the meeting, sitting
quietly. As soon as it was over, and we were outside the
church building, he hurried to the Pathan's side, and
started speaking very loudly to him, demanding to know
if he was becoming a Christian. 'Tell me! Tell me!'
Ahmed Ghul said, 'I am a Christian!' The Kohati cajoled
and threatened him, 'You are a Nasrani! A kafir! A
heretic! An infidel! You had better give up such an idea.
If you do not I shall spread the news all over Kohat that
you, Ahmed Ghul, a Pathan, are a Christian. And it is
not only you who will suffer, but also the sahib here, and
I do not think that he will be willing to pay the price
with you.' Ahmed looked at me and asked me, 'Will you
be willing, sahib, to stand with me as a Christian, and
pay the price if need be?' I said that I would. A sense of
relief and joy lit up the face of our dear friend. 'Do you
hear that?' he asked the young man. 'The sahib will go all
the way with me. You have your answer. Go in peace.' I
also wished him well. But my heart was heavy as we
descended the hill.

We felt that it would not be wise and right to have him
much longer with us, but that we should soon receive him
into our church fellowship and get him away that very
day to his own 'quam,' or people. We felt he would be
safer there than with us. He could return to us, now and
again, when he wanted to do so. There would always be
a warm welcome for him. It was arranged that at a Sunday afternoon service he should tell of his faith in the

Saviour, and of how he became a Christian. He would speak in his own Pashto, and his testimony would be translated into Urdu and English. Plans were made that immediately afterwards a Pakistani brother and I would set off with him, I going so far and returning, and the two of them going on much farther towards Ahmed's own people among the hills, when our Pakistani friend would return to us.

But the Sunday of the meeting was a disturbed one. During the morning a group of Pathans arrived at the home of the lady-missionaries. Evidently men of some consequence, as shown by their manner and dress, they asked to speak with Ahmed Ghul who came out to them, and a spokesman of the group said to him, 'Ahmed Ghul, old man of our people, we have heard that you are leaving the religion of your fathers, and turning to another religion, thereby becoming an infidel with whom we may deal severely. But we respect your age and want to give you every chance to remain a Moslem. Will you now repeat the Qualima, and renounce Christ?' There was silence. The brightly attired group of Moslem citizens waited for Ahmed to speak. Their leader held out an apparently generous handful of money to our brave friend, saying, 'Return to your faith, and you can have all this I have in my hand. There is enough here to keep you in comfort for quite a long time to come. Refuse and you become an infidel, an apostate from the true faith. Return, Ahmed Ghul! Repent and return!' He made the grand refusal that Sunday morning. 'I am a Christian,' he said. 'And though you were to offer me a hundred times the money in your hand. I shall never return from following after Christ.' Warning Ahmed Ghul of what might happen to him they went away. Miss Davidson and Miss Rasmussen gave me the account of this.

That afternoon with an eager and ready gladness he stood by my side, and in his throaty gutterals and the rolling r's of his Pashto, testified to having assurance of forgiveness of sin and everlasting life through faith in Christ Jesus. We praised and prayed, sang our psalms, and rejoiced with Ahmed in his delight in the Lord. It was a touching and sacred moment when we committed him to the Lord God of the threshold, who blesses the goings out and comings in of His children. We saw to his having nourishment before he set off, and sustenance for the way, and the three of us went off together. Reaching my parting place with Ahmed we exchanged our farewells. My last word to him was the Pashto word of the parting of friends, 'May good go before you!' In the Pathan tongue, 'Pah mache de khah.' I stood watching him till they disappeared from my sight. The goodness of God went before him. His goodness and mercy followed him. He dwells in the house of the Lord for ever. He never came again to us. We could not go to him.

37: *A frontier fellowship*

It will be readily seen that the Urdu word 'kalisiya', for church, comes from the Greek 'ecclesia.' And in our 'kalisiya' in Kohat there were some notable characters, in their own way, as well as others more ordinary, who plodded on quietly, living their humble lives, and leaving us for their eternal Home when their day's work was done. It was a sad enough task, helping to get a coffin ready for one such, the mortal frame lying nearby in the

sunshine. The humble in life, the humble in death, represented most of our fellowship and congregation.

Others were better known. Faquira among them, an
elder, highly esteemed for godly living, a prayerful, pleasant man who had escaped out of scavenging into being,
in a small way, a cloth merchant. Wise in church affairs
he often gave evidence that his wisdom was the peaceable
wisdom from above. Fellowship reached a new dimension
between him and me when he asked me if I would care to
become a partner with him in his small business when I
returned to Britain! This I could not do. But he himself
continued in his 'kapri,' or cloth affairs until he was
clothed with immortality.

Atu, his wife and family, lived close by, not many doors
from my own 'door', which was that of a big room we
had used as a place of worship before our church building
was erected. When I was out, birds occupied it, and I had
to 'shoo' them out on returning. A stone behind the door
was its only lock! And there were holes for the birds to
enter when they chose! There was no means of locking it
from the outside so others could enter when they chose.
Outside, orioles and paroquets darted about in gold and
green. Atu had a nice young family, and, naturally
enough, sometimes one of them was unwell, which meant
I was called upon for advice, or even to do some poultic-
ing! And this in the night! I was easily reached. And so
was all I had, as I found one day, when Atu invited me
to a meal with him and his family. The buffalo-dung
cakes plastered the outside walls of his humble home. The
patient buffaloes whisked their useful tails at the myriads
of flies as I was welcomed in. A table was set with knives,
forks and spoons! I was surprised for I knew he had no
cutlery. On a closer look at them I thought that they
rather resembled my own. I laughed! So did Atu! They

were my own! 'Well,' he said, 'how could we invite you here to eat with us and no cutlery for you to use? We went round to your house for it this morning when you were out.' Atu was a scavenger, a sweeper, ever at work among filth, human and animal. Fellowship! I was glad to live beside them.

Between Atu's home and mine was that of Masih Das, an earnest and hard-working pastor, a man with a deep understanding of his own people. He led our services from a slightly higher vantage point from the rest of us who sat on the floor and he often asked me to strike up the psalm, or 'bhajan.' These lovely Punjabi tunes! Beautiful! They often suffered through my beginning them too high or too low. His own high-pitched voice was an asset, here, there and everywhere.

Our church planting in Kohat was a pioneer effort, the aim being a self-supporting church fellowship with a pastor and kirk-session, on which I served as an elder. There were the lady-missionaries, Miss Davidson and Miss Rasmussen, and we were in the American Presbytery of the Punjab. Moneys saved for the new church building were in the hands of Masih Das, the pastor. And one day things took a very serious turn for him and for us. An American colleague had arrived from the Punjab Presbytery. I found him sitting near my door looking rather tried and disconsolate, and asked him if there was anything wrong. 'A great deal,' he said. 'I have been inquiring from Masih Das about the moneys he has been in charge of to help to begin the building of the new place, but he says he has none!' I asked why. 'Well', he said, 'Masih Das says that he has been lending sums from the Post Office account to those who wished to borrow from him, with the promise that they would repay with interest before the building commenced, and they have not done so.' All this had been going on, and I knew nothing about it. We were teaching self-support, and left as much as possible in the hands of the nationals. Rather a difficult part of my job was to have him, the pastor, adequately supported. This was a blow to us all.

Poor blamable Masih Das! He and I set off by train one bright morning to be present at the Presbytery Meeting in Rawalpindi. There would be a representative group from the Punjab, ministers, missionaries, pastors and elders, and we two from the Frontier. My companion did not seem unduly concerned, and in his kindness had brought a blind man with him to meet some relatives and friends. His view was that he had helped others, and they had promised to repay with interest. He had not expected the moneys to be needed so soon. Indiscreet, he maintained, he may have been, but he had not acted wrongfully. My own view was that he should not have loaned the moneys. They were not his. To some extent I realised that I was in an environment with a heritage of action different from my own. A well-meaning friend had advised me to study psychology that I might the better understand the minds of the Asiatic people among whom I ministered. My answer was that I would understand them better by praying for them. I could learn most about them by waiting upon God for them – for those from Islam and Hinduism with minds renewed in Christ, and for those whose minds were blind and could not yet see, and who were still in these systems. My helps would be the Holy Spirit and the Holy Scriptures.

The Presbytery conducted the case of Masih Das in Urdu. Several of us, including myself, had to speak. My own position was unique. He and I had to travel back together, live next door to each other and serve as one in Christ's cause on the Frontier. We had to keep in the love of God, and the unity of the Spirit. The debate was serious enough. Masih Das simply said all he could say. Almost to a man those of the East stood with him in his viewpoint over his action. We of the West felt that he had acted unwisely and wrongfully, and the moneys which were not his were now lost. The nationals won the case for him. They maintained that we non-nationals did not understand life within the Indian Church. Masih Das was absolved from all fault and wrong except for indiscretion in church affairs. On the whole there was a sense of disappointment among us. One rather amusing moment for me was when a fellow-missionary, a Britisher, in the Presbytery, quietly stood to his feet and said nothing. The Americans and Indians wondered what this meant, but it soon dawned on them as it had dawned on me. A military band in the vicinity was playing the National Anthem. I did not stand up; it would have spoiled the occasion.

Away we went next morning on the train for the Frontier, Masih Das, his blind friend and myself, carrying our gourds of water for the journey. I never made reference again to the mismanagement of the building moneys. The building began, and day by day saw advance in it. We felt that it would be in keeping with the surroundings to have a modest-sized white dome above the portico of the main door. It fell in the first time of erection. But not the second time! The great day came when, 'forsaking not the assembling of ourselves together', we passed under it to worship the Lord while the bell pealed out its cheerful welcome.

Many of the people who came about the church were of low caste Hindu stock – something of which Islam knows nothing, since all are equal in it – and were nominally Christian, but showing little of the power of Christ

[159]

in their lives. They had become Christians, so called, to escape their low caste stigma. We saw them as sick souls in dire need of His healing. Our work was to lead them to faith in Christ. Even then, their lives were a challenge to us to lead them into deeper spiritual living.

Such a challenge was Charan Yusuf. He made a profession of faith in Christ when he and I were having Bible lessons. Regretfully, he was addicted to the drug 'hashshish,' or 'bhang', made from the tops and sprouts of Indian hemp. I took him on to cook for me, and to help him in the faith. Sometimes I had to go supperless to my bed while Charan lay in one of his pathetic stupors. Careless and foolish he often was! One morning he brought in my pot of tea, and when I poured from it, the cup began to fill with dead monster ants! Smaller species had sweet times in the sugar! One night he came running for me, saying that he and a friend had been attacked by three men. It was so! I was ready for bed, but had to go out to the rescue, pyjama-clad. Charan certainly represented some of the material in our congregation. They were the lowest in the land, but one never tired of telling them that by faith in the Lord Jesus Christ they could become sons of God, and daughters of the Almighty.

Eventually Charan got a job with a military man, and stayed in a small room next door to mine. One morning, I did not hear him go out to his work, and wondered why. He had lost his job. He had not made the grade. By what he told me, my fellow-country people, man and wife, did not make the grade either. According to Charan they were better when they were drunk, but they were very rude and unkind to him when they were sober, actually hitting and kicking him, besides withholding wages from him. This I could not accept, and got into touch with them. In spite of all Charan's limitations they were going rather too far in their unkind treatment of him. They were not very pleasant people, and it seemed to me they were like fools riding upon horses, who could not have acted so at home, in Britain. We had a number of them, besides many who were a credit to their country. I spoke to a high-ranking officer about the matter and he asked me to put the case forward to him, and he would see that the soldier was reduced to the ranks. This I declined to do, but I let the offenders know what my mind was on the matter. When my time to leave Kohat came, Charan was there among those, who, with their touch of gold, bade me farewell, one of the very weak who bore His Name!

38: *False witnesses*

The Moslems of Baltistan are Shiahs like those of Iran, and are considered to be heretical by orthodox Sunnis, such as the Moslems of Afghanistan. The division between them is over who was successor to Muhammad, who died rather suddenly leaving the Koran unfinished. The succession was undecided. There were three claimants, Ali, who was married to Fatima, a daughter of Muhammad; Omar; and a third who gave up his claim in favour of the others. Those who were considered to be orthodox were for Omar who was murdered shortly afterwards, as was the man who followed him. Abu Bakr, Muhammad's father-in-law, held the position of Caliph for a time, but a strong party was for Ali. This led to bitter strife, and to the two permanent divisions in Islam, the Sunni, or People of the Law, and the Shiah, or People of the Party.

There is also a third grouping now in Islam, the Ahmadiya, Qadian, or New Messiah, founded by Mirza Ghulam Ahmed Khan, who was born in the village of Qadian, Punjab, in 1839, but who is considered unsound in Islam by both Shiah and Sunni, although, when his celebrated work *Ahmadiya Proofs* appeared it was well received. A Qadiani is today apt to be looked upon, especially by a Sunni, as a heretic. Christian, Jew and Moslem look for a coming Messiah. Mirza Ahmad claimed Messiahship, and went so far as to claim that the grave of the Lord Jesus Christ had been found in Kashmir, saying that the Saviour did not ascend up into heaven, but up into the Himalaya and died there. The Ahmadiya now have a mosque in Woking, England.

On our fields of service we found the Qadian willing to exchange points of view, both in talking with us, and by correspondence. They usually reason from a Koranic point of view when in dialogue with a Christian, and from a Biblical one when differing with another Moslem. However scholarly and well-meaning Mirza Ahmad was, the Christian cannot accept his philosophy of religion, nor the revelations he claimed to have. Mirza Ahmad's writings are informative and interesting, showing a knowledge of men, religion, books and things, but his philosophy of religion, and the revelations which he claimed to have received are far removed from the Christian Scriptures and the Gospel of the Lord Jesus Christ.

The Ahmadiya or Quadian outlook is being severely challenged in some quarters of Pakistan by orthodox Islam, and a number of that way have lost their lives. The Government has preserved the lives of others, whereas there are those who want them to be outlawed and even executed. It is a time when Pakistan is faced with an angry Afghanistan which, besides its push to get rid of foreigners, is claiming that the Pathans are Afghanis, and that their country, Pakhtunistan is part of Afghanistan. But equally firmly, N.W. Pakistan says that she will not have her territory torn apart, and would possibly go to war about it if need be.

A Qadian brought Rex Bavington and myself a book to read on the Ahmadiya Movement. We felt that the best thing to do would be to review it in his presence. All to its disadvantage. It contained absurd statements about Mirza Ahmad such as that he had fulfilled what Christ had said about the elect being gathered by the angels from the four winds. This happened in a town in North India. Mirza had sent out people all over it to call them to a meeting at which he would speak, thereby fulfilling the prophecy. Then again, the Lord Jesus Christ raised up the daughter of Jairus from death, having said, 'she is not dead but sleepeth.' Mirza Ahmad had also done this when people were thought to be dead, but were only asleep! Our well-meaning friend admitted that Quadian claims in such a fashion for the Messiahship of Mirza were rather far-fetched. We spoke with this friend face to face but correspondence can be a worthwhile method in missionary work, and knowing this we had an exchange of letters with an Ahmadiya secretary in Lahore.

Other correspondents come to mind, such as a Britisher caught up in Islam. Jubilant Moslems came bragging about this soldier who had become one of them. Getting into touch with him I invited him to come and see me. This he would not do. We wrote to each other, and he said that in Britain he had attended worship, been a Sunday School teacher, and a Christian, but all had been of no use to him. I had to point out to him that probably

[163]

he had only been a Christian in name, and had not been born again, thereby becoming a partaker of the divine nature, and that he was now just the same as he had ever been, whether he bore the name of Christian or Moslem.

There were British soldiers serving in the North-West Frontier Province who bore steady witness to the saving power of the Lord Jesus Christ. A ministry in which I had a part was a Bible Class for British soldiers. It is a joy to remember soldiers who later became ministers and pastors, and another who served in the London City Mission. We could look in, too, to see patients in the Military Hospital, and have a reading of Scripture and prayer with them. One experience there caused me great regret. While I was speaking to a Christian soldier, another soldier in the next bed to him, hearing my accent, spoke up saying that he came from near my home. He was quite ill, though he himself said that he did not know what his illness was. Leaving the ward that day, at the hospital door I felt that I should go back and have a fur- ther word about salvation with him. I did not go. The following Sunday, when one or two soldiers and myself were going to the Bible Class we heard bugles sounding the Last Post. I asked whose funeral it was. They told me. It was that of the friend with whom I should have spoken.

In those days in India there were ministers among the European people, and chaplains in the Forces who gave the message of the saving power of Christ. There were others who evidently did not. This occasioned distress to sincere believers in the Lord Jesus Christ, for example a sergeant whom I went to speak with in the regimental lines. He had been voluntarily at a service in the Canton- ments, and had been shocked and disappointed. When I went to see him the sentry in the lines challenged me. I told him who I was and whom I wanted to see, namely the sergeant of his guard. When he came out, he said, 'Oh, it's you. I thought it was the clergyman from the Cantonments. I am hoping that he will come to see me. The sentry simply said that that padre chap had come to see me, and I thought that it was he.' When I asked him what had happened, he told me that he had gone to the service on Sunday evening, and the chaplain had preached a sermon on what he called, 'The Five B's That Built Britain.' The five were Beef, Brawn, Brains, Beer and the Bible. High-ranking officers and non-commissioned officers were present. When he came to speak about the Bible building Britain, 'Of course', he said, 'when I am speaking about the Bible I am not referring to the Old Testament. I am not a believer in the Old Testament.' At this, the sergeant rose up in his pew, came out into the aisle, and marched down to the door, every head turning to look at him, and went out into the open air. He added, 'I await the chaplain coming to see me. I shall tell him that if a chaplain does not believe the Word of God, an ordinary serving soldier does believe it.'

The beneficial rule of the British was often quite apparent, as was the worth of the army, on the Frontier. We missionaries were in a world apart. Even so things would filter through to us, such as hearing a Pathan piper playing 'The Cock o' the North,' at a Khattock clan wedding; a bunch of Ghurkas marching past playing, 'Hielan Laddie,' and a lone flute player in the early morning playing, 'Auld Lang Syne.' But our world was mostly one of savagery and simplicity where, very much alone, we served the Crucified and Risen Saviour. Fanciful things were believed by the folks around us, such as the wonder of the 'growing grave'. It was that of a Moslem holy man who was said to grow in his grave! How was this known? It was known because there were more white

stones around it than there were the last time it was
visited! It grew until it came to the edge of the public
road, and then the powers that be said, 'thus far and no
farther.'

39: Lady missionary colleagues

There are not many books about Christian missionary
work in the North-West Frontier Province, now part of
North-West Pakistan. Two of those which should be read
are: *Hidden Highway* and *Wild Frontier,* both by Flora
Davidson, one of the most devoted of missionaries who
knew the Pathan people as no one else has possibly ever
done, and who served among them for over forty years.
Privileged to serve for a short time with her and her colleague, Maria Rasmussen, I knew Miss Davidson quite
well, and saw some of her works of faith and labours of
love, and still have the journals and diaries left to me
when she died.

The two ladies lived in Kohat City, unguarded and
alone, except for Mir Baz, an Afridi Pathan, who would
have given his life for the Mem Sahibs, but who would
not let his son come under the influence of the Gospel, or
even be educated at primary level, lest he should not feel
like revenging his father if Mir Baz was injured or killed
in a blood feud. Both ladies were dedicated to the Lord
Jesus, body, mind and spirit, and would have been faithful unto death, if need be. Sometimes Miss Davidson
slept at night fully clothed, when there were rumours of a
kidnapping taking place. She hoped that she would be

taken away into the fastnesses of the hills so that she could be among people who had never heard the Gospel. She was a brave woman, generous and humorous, with a laugh that reminded one of the pealing of a bell. Both were fluent in Pashto and Urdu and were at home with men, women and children. They ministered day and night, witnessing for Christ through dispensary work and hospitality to tribal people, earning an esteem incredible in such a fanatically Moslem environment. Staunch in fellowship, and wise in counsel because of their fuller experience, I was ever glad of their words of wisdom and of knowledge.

One day a man dressed in the saffron robes of a Hindu Sadhu came to see me. He told a remarkable story of his conversion to Christ. I listened enthralled as we sat and drank tea together. As he came to the close of his seemingly true testimony he asked that he should be baptised, and said he was quite willing to be baptised anywhere, in the 'girja' (church building), or in the open, as soon as possible, and that he would then move away to another part of the country, with maybe a little money, and we could prayerfully wish him well. Telling him that I would confer with my fellow-missionaries, and be back as quickly as I could, I left him in my home, and dashed away to speak with Miss Davidson and Miss Rasmussen, who listened to me with evident interest, but showed no enthusiasm at all about what I told them. Their cool attitude puzzled me, and I was startled when Flora Davidson said, 'We have heard all this before. You go back and tell him that he cannot be baptised just now. Advise him to stay with us for a time, and prove to us that he is a sincere believer on the Lord Jesus Christ. He can then be baptised, and received into the church fellowship.' I was neither pleased nor convinced. With such a testimony as I had listened to I could see nothing to hinder the man from being baptised. 'This is ridiculous,' I said. 'Here we are working day and night to bring people to Christ, and when a man comes along and tells us that the Holy Spirit has moved him to believe on the Lord Jesus Christ, and wants to go on further with Him, we are the very ones to discourage him from doing so.' They smiled, saying, 'Jock, we have been here longer than you have, and have heard all this story before. We know by what you have told us that this man is a fraud. You will soon know this too.' Somewhat disgusted I returned to the saffron-robed one and told him what my fellow-missionaries had said.

I was unprepared for his reactions. He was furious, and fell into a temper unbelievable to see and hear from one who had said that he was a new creation in Christ. He called all of us by most odious names. I remonstrated with him, and tried to calm him down, but without success. A Christian may be able in some circumstances to shake the dust from off his feet! He could not! He stirred up enough to envelop himself and us completely. Raging fiercely, after I had given him a little money to help him on his travel, he left me to get my breath back, have a wash, and set out to see the lady-missionaries, apologise to them, and have a short time of fellowship together over a cup of tea. What had happened was all part of the work, for us the most important work in the world. Sometime later we heard of this strange man, purporting to be a Christian sadhu, who had been baptised in quite a number of places, and received financial help wherever he went. In fact, he was an often-baptised man in different parts of the sub-continent before he came to us. But even multiple baptism is not Christ and his salvation.

Our Evangelistic Campaign Week, held every now and again, needed thought and spiritual preparation. Everyone was expected to take part. There were special services in the 'girja' and the womenfolk were in it too, though most of these were very poor and illiterate. There was also Gospel literature distribution, though when that had begun in Kohat City, a mullah threatened Miss Davidson, saying that on the giving of the first piece of Christian literature she would be killed. Impudently some would come leering at us, tearing up the booklets and tracts in front of us. Miss Davidson once gave a cheeky boy a mild smack for doing so. Many of those we spoke with spat on the ground whenever we mentioned the Name of the Lord Jesus. Sometimes I had to wipe their spittle from my face. We were there in His Name, and by His grace we honoured it.

A valued part of my missionary possessions are the journals and diaries of Miss Davidson left to me when she died. There are also personal letters. When she returned to her post for the last time she wrote, 'I am just off again, break of day, and do need your prayer help. I'm rather dreading it all again. You know what it all means. But the yellow light flashed and now the green is on, so go I must. It was good seeing you again. Maybe next time it will be in the air, with Him, higher than the 'planes go, and no coming down! As you know, I did not want to get better, or go on – but last Sunday, at the breaking of bread His wonderful love came over me once again and I'm glad, if I have something to give though only the dregs ... blessings on you ... Flora Davidson.' The dregs of what? The master-missionary furnishes the answer. The dregs of a life poured out in His Name for the salvation of others, 'Yea, and if I be offered – poured out upon the sacrifice of your faith, I joy, and rejoice with you all.

For the same cause also do ye joy, and rejoice with me.'
As with Paul the apostle, so with Flora Davidson, and I
told her so. But she was able to return to Britain, and was
sometimes with my wife and myself at WEC H.Q., in our
home, and at missionary meetings. We were getting ready
to go out again to N.-W. Pakistan, when we were asked to
serve on our British Home Staff, on which we serve at
present. Flora served on her field until she could serve no
longer, and having had an accident, retired to a Home
where I used to go to be with her, talk about the Frontier,
the work of the Lord there, and pray.

40: *Open air witness*

Our 'Bahir Gawahi,' or 'Open Air Witness,' of which I
was in charge, was not an easy assignment. I usually
awoke from my sleep on the day of the proposed meetings
thinking of what could happen to me in them, and to
any others who might accompany me. My rise and fall of
spirit made me examine myself as to whether I had been
called to be a missionary of the Gospel or no. With many
in our fellowship coming from low caste Hinduism –
Harijan, or 'children of Vishnu,' as Mahatma Gandhi
had, with good intention, called them – it was a thing unheard of that they should go out into the open air in such
a place as Kohat, and witness for Christ. To the Moslems,
and high caste Hindus, they were as the dust beneath
their feet, even their shadow being despicable. Those who
knew Christ had the knowledge that they were children
of God by faith in Christ Jesus, and we ever told them so.
But that did not take away their holding back from going

out among the warlike and the powerful. Most of them were ignorant of letters. For us they were the worshippers of 'Hariyala Bana', or The Fair Bridegroom, Christ Jesus. They humbly bore His Name among the proud around them. Segregated in their own living-quarters, a 'mahalla', were numbers of families, many dogs and hardworking patient buffaloes standing by or lying at rest. Buffalo dung, made up into cakes, formed the fuel of the fires. Jammed to the doors were our meetings in a home there in a 'mahalla'. Hardly able to breathe, it seemed, in the heat and stench, it made me wonder how we managed to praise and pray as we did. But to come out and witness among the Pathans, and the high-born Hindus, there was not the power, through lack of desire, fear, and the feeling that it was not worthwhile.

The procedure for the open air witness was, first of all, a time of prayer before setting out. I usually was the only one who turned up for that, but I did not think harshly of my friends. It was tough enough for me, more so for them, and I knew many of them were thinking of me.

After prayer, we, or more usually myself, set off for a selected place where there was enough room for a crowd to collect. Often this was opposite the main gate into the city. I would begin by reading aloud parts of the Holy Scriptures, often parts of the first three chapters of the Epistle to the Romans. Some heard what the Word of God had to say about man in need of a Saviour. Hardly anyone might be about, but as soon as I began to read, men and boys gathered from all directions, hemming me in. The usual thing was that they listened for a little while, and then began to hurl questions at me, a familiar one being, 'Do you eat pig?' The answer to that one was that I did not. There was applause for that. But it was for their sakes I did not eat pig, for it would have meant interminable unimportant arguments about eating pig, and not eating it. Besides pig could not be had! Someone would follow on with, 'Do you drink wine?' The answer again was in the negative. Interest mounted, as did the cries, 'Well done! Well done! You are almost a Moslem.' A difficult question was, 'Why is it written in your Scriptures, "Ye are gods?"' In a language not my own the like of that was not easy to answer. The crowd would ever grow bigger, and more clamant.

I would ask permission from them to read to them more passages from the Bible. This granted, there was silence again, but only for a time. Seeking to reach their consciences I would read to them what the Saviour said about man becoming defiled, not by what entered his stomach, but by what came out of his heart. Some thoughtfully seemed to accept this indictment of themselves, and said nothing. Others looked glum and annoyed. Others became angry, and shouted abuse at me. Soon a spokesman for them was pouring out the teachings of Islam, and haranguing me at the same time. Sometimes I managed to smile, and to say above the din, 'I say, sir, this is my meeting.' The reply was given with a triumphant laugh, 'Not at all! Not at all! You have now lost it. It is ours! Ask any questions you like!' By this time I did not feel like asking any questions, but just listened. The peace of God kept my heart, but sometimes there was the question being asked within me as to whether this was the right way of witnessing to the Gospel. Amid the hubbub of raucous cries in support of Muhammad and Islam, I would slip away home when I could. One evening a lad did manage a direct hit with a stone, between my shoulder blades.

But things could really get out of hand at these meetings. One was glad to see National Police hovering around with their small batons handy. One night the fires of antagonism burned fiercely, and the Qualima, harsh and uncompromising, doubly heated them. I stood looking at the shouting mob. And then it happened! There was a rush towards me. Fists shook and hands stretched out to grab me. Police ran to get between them and me and succeeded in beating the mob off with their short sticks. But the pressure was so fierce that we were driven across the road, in through the main gate, and up into the bazaar. I felt both insulted and assaulted, to say the least. Still, one lived on from day to day. Godly Faquaira came to see me, apologising for not going with me to the 'bahir gawahi', saying, 'We are so poor and weak, sahib, we cannot go. I watch you from a distance all the time of the meeting. You must give up this open air work. It is too dangerous. I have followed you home at times. But I regret to tell you that one night I saw another man follow you home and he had a knife.'

All things considered, we felt it was not wise to go on with the public open air witness. Donald Fullerton being with me for a time, we went out on personal work instead. The usual procedure was to go into the bazaar, and talk with anyone who was willing to talk with us. Donald did most of this with anyone who could speak English. I did with anyone who spoke Urdu, with a smattering of Pashto. While one engaged in conversation the other stood by, praying silently. This we found was a more satisfactory way of working in the open, though small crowds would collect wherever we were. There were never more than minor difficulties; most of those we spoke with were shopkeepers, who always had an eye for business. We were a sort of advertisement for them.

41: By love constrained

Evangelical missionary efforts on the east and west Afghan frontiers should be better known by the church of God. The Afghan Border Crusade, Central Asian Mission, Church Missionary Society, American Presbyterians, Worldwide Evangelization Crusade and other missions share in the missionary enterprise there. They are worthy of prayerful interest. Men and women on these frontiers live devoted lives for the sake of the Gospel, caring for orphans, medical work and educational work, mission farm work and other forms of approach to the unevangelized in these needy regions. It is all made possible by missionary-hearted Christians who have prayed and given, often sacrificially.

One is reminded of what practical love is, in the missionary cause, by a plaque above a bed in a ward of the Church Missionary Society Hospital, in Peshawar, which tells that the bed was given and endowed by the sister of Captain Arthur Connolly in the prayerful hope that it might be beneficial to Pathans, the nearest people reachable, and of the same religion as the people who had so cruelly murdered her brother. It moves one reading it, to stand by the bed speaking to the patient, usually a Pathan tribesman, suffering, like most of the others in the ward, from feud wounds.

Colonel Stoddart and Captain Connolly were lawfully representing their country in Bokhara in Uzbekistan, near the Oxus River, when the Amir arrested them, and threw them into a loathsome prison infested with vermin and reptiles that gnawed the flesh from their bones. They were offered life and freedom if they would say the Qualima, and become Moslems. It was said of Stoddart that through fear he had said it, but that, soon after he withdrew what he had said, and avowed that he was a Christian. Joseph Wolff in his Journal *Mission to Bokhara*, says that the Khan, a high-ranking Moslem personage, said to him, 'Both Captain Connolly and Colonel Stoddart were brought, with their hands tied, behind the Ark (palace) in the presence of Makram Saadat, when Colonel Stoddart and Captain Connolly kissed each other, and Colonel Stoddart said to Saadat, "Tell the Amir that I die a disbeliever in Muhammad, but a believer in Jesus; that I am a Christian, and a Christian I die." And Connolly said, "Stoddart, we shall see each other in Paradise, near Jesus." Saadat then gave the order to cut off, first the head of Stoddart, which was done; and in the same manner the head of Connolly was cut off.' Joseph Wolff looked upon them as true Christian martyrs.

The hazardous journey and perilous search for Connolly and Stoddart by Joseph Wolff, missionary to Jews and Moslems, is one of the most absorbing and thrilling stories in missionary history. In Bokhara, Wolff himself was imprisoned in the filthy cell in which the two soldiers were held before they were executed, and a leading mullah was sent to ask him to deny Christ and become a Moslem. In his Journal he recounts that he told the mullah to go back and tell the Amir that his answer was, 'Never! Never! Never!' A few hours later the executioner of Stoddart and Connolly came saying, 'Joseph Wolff, to you it shall happen as it did to Stoddart and Connolly,' and he made a sign with his hand across Wolff's throat. Says Wolff, 'I prepared for death and carried opium about with me, in case my throat was cut that I might not feel the pain. However, at last, I cast away the opium and prayed, and wrote in my Bible these words, 'My Dearest Georgiana and Henry, I have loved you both unto death. Your affectionate husband and father, J. Wolff.' On the day of his planned execution there came a messenger from Muhammad Shah, Ruler of Persia, demanding Wolff's release, or the consequences might be serious. On reading the letter the Amir of Bokhara said to the messenger, 'Well, I make a present to you of Joseph Wolff. He may go with you.' With the envoy from Persia Wolff set off on the beginning of his long, tiring journey by foot and horse through Persia, the country of his rescuer, to Turkey, then on to Greece, and by boat to Malta, to Gibraltar and London, bringing with him the moving news of the Christian witness and martyr deaths of Stoddart and Connolly. It is one of the finest stories known of heroic missionary endeavour. Wolff, an Oriental scholar and minister of Christ, fulfilled the work of an evangelist, appearing before European lords and ladies, Eastern kings, rulers, and Moslem mullahs of all grades, often at severe cost.

Some months after the death of Joseph Wolff a small parcel was brought to Mrs Frances MacNaughton, the sister of Captain Connolly. In it was a soiled and battered copy of the Book of Common Prayer which had been brought from Bokhara to Russia, and from there by interested Poles to London. Regrettably, it is now lost, but the notes that were in it were copied from the fly-leaves and margins, and have been preserved. In it Connolly had written, 'Thank God that this book was left to me. Stoddart and I have found it a great comfort. We did not know before this affliction what was in the Psalms, or how beautiful are the prayers of our church. Desiring that the circumstances of our last treatment at Bokhara should become known, and conceiving that a record made in this book has a better chance of preservation than one made upon loose paper, I herein note the chief occurrences since my arrival.' It is a diary of a thousand words, and a will, and ends in the middle of a sentence as if Connolly had been interrupted while writing. Stoddart and Connolly were soldiers and comported themselves so; but they were also good soldiers of Jesus Christ, and in their dreadful imprisonment, torture and death, endured, had faith, talked about Him, believed on His Name, and lived to His praise right to the end. There was one who also endured much, hoping to find them alive, help them, and bring them home again, Joseph Wolff, missionary. Whatever the feelings of horror, sorrow and respair which overwhelmed Mrs MacNaughton, sister of Captain Connolly, when she had the tragic news about him and his friend, Colonel Stoddart, the love of Christ constrained her to endow a bed in the C.M.S. Hospital in Peshawar where many a sick and wounded tribesman has rested and heard the Gospel. It was as near as she could get to Bokhara.

42: *Homeward bound incidents*

When my return to Britain drew near I carried my boatfare in a belted pouch in the small of my back. While in Baltistan we each carried ten golden sovereigns in case of emergency, but never had occasion to use them. The people of Lesser Thibet would accept nothing but the Indian rupee. For safe keeping it was the best I could do. One evening Rex and I went for a walk and talk near Peshawar, and met a man with some water buffaloes who looked aghast at us and asked us where we were going. We told him we were just having a walk. 'Go back! Go back!' he said. 'You do not know whom you are going to meet up there. But I do. Go back at once.' Rex asked me if I had any money with me, and I said that I had my boat-fare. It was in the usual place. 'Come on! Come on!' he said, 'Let's get back home at once!' Thanking the buffalo man we lost no time in returning to the home of the Bavingtons in the city.

The journey from the Frontier was uneventful. I met a fellow-countryman in Rawalpindi who said that he wondered why we stayed in that country except to make money. I told him that I made no money, but had a better job. I was a missionary of the Gospel! Words appeared to fail him! It is quite a rail journey to Bombay, and from Rawalpindi, during part of it, a young man, rather likable too, singled me out as a target for his stinging epithets, for what he felt were the faults and crimes of British imperial rule. At a station where we got out for a breather he gathered a crowd around him, and directed their attention on me. It was an unpleasant situation, but having lived among Pathans it did not trouble me much. My concern was to comport myself as a servant of Christ, and this by His help I was able to do. It was but another opportunity to witness among some of them to the saving power of the Lord Jesus, and there was satisfaction to me in that. At Delhi I gave a man some money to get some eatables for me before the train went out but he never came back!

In Bombay Railway Station I was having a bath after the three-day railway journey, and was getting on very well with it, when outside the door a stentorian British voice demanded that I hurry up, for he, whoever he was, wanted a bath too. This was emphasised by a thudding on the door by what sounded like a hefty fist. I said that I would not be long but I occasionally got a wild shout, and a heavy bang on the door to speed me up. When I came out there stood before me, stripped to the waist like a heavyweight boxer, one of the biggest men I had seen since leaving the Frontier. 'Have a cigarette,' he said. Thanking him I declined it, saying that I did not smoke. 'Come and have a drink then.' He seemed now in no hurry for his bath! I told him that I did not drink. This was too much for him. Swearing, he asked me who I thought I was to refuse his tokens of friendliness. I quietly told him that I was no one in particular but just an ordinary Scotsman. He roared at me, 'Do you mean to tell me that Scotsmen do not smoke and drink?' Telling him that I meant no such thing, I politely let him know that I was one who neither smoked tobacco nor took strong drink. 'What are you then?' he demanded. 'I am a Christian missionary,' I said. This was again just too much for him. He shouted across into the waiting room where two Britishers were seated at a table with what was evidently a big bottle of whisky between them, 'Look at this, boys. Here is a missionary!' He laughed uproariously in sarcasm. But it was my turn now. The two at the table listened as I told their big friend of the wonderful joy of being a Christian, and of how proud I was of being a Christian missionary, a servant of the Lord Jesus Christ, and that it was the greatest thing in the world to be His and to serve Him. I then spoke to him of his need of the Saviour, and asked him what he was going to do about it. He made a dash for the bathroom door, slammed it fast, and locked it. With a word to the other men I left the Railway Station.

Having a day to spare before the boat sailed, I moved around talking to various folks, particularly Parsees, or

Zoroastrians, some of whose forbears met David Livingstone when he arrived in Bombay, where he sold his river-
boat the 'Lady Nyasa', having piloted it, with his few
African crewmen, across the Indian Ocean because it was
too deep of keel to use on the farther reaches of the River
Zambezi. He then went back to Central Africa and his
visit was remembered among the Parsee community in
Bombay. When Livingstone's birthplace in Blantyre, Lan-
arkshire was restored and made into the David Livingstone Memorial, they subscribed gifts of money for a
painting of his ship the 'Lady Nyasa' to hang there.

During the day I met one of the two men whom I had
seen with the bottle of whisky in the waiting-room. We
stood and spoke together. He asked for money which I
said I could not give him after seeing him and the others
with the alcohol. 'Yes,' he said, 'that stuff belonged to the
big man, the retired policeman from Calcutta; but my
friend and I never touched a drop of it. We dared not.
Our stomachs were so empty.' On my asking him if the
'big man' had given them anything for food he said that
he had not. All this, of course, may, or may not have been
true. I gave him a few rupees, and at his request, agreed to
meet him and his friend, and talk with them before the
boat sailed. We met, and I took them to a restaurant for
some food. They gave me their history. They both had
had worthwhile jobs but their lives and prospects had
been ruined by drink and bad company. We spoke together of the Saviour, sin and salvation. Again they had
a few rupees, and when the time came one of them carried
my baggage to the ship, and my last hours in Asia were
spent with these two down-and-out British tramps who
lived in some old disused railway carriages near Bombay
docks. It seemed strange to me as I stood waving them
goodbye from the deck of the liner, after having been so

far away in the Himalaya, the Karakoram and the Khyber Hills, that my final evangelistic efforts should be with two of my own nation.

43: *They went over, the trumpets sounding*

After about a year doing some further studies, and working as a home missionary of the Church of Scotland, I had a severe spinal injury while travelling as a passenger in a car. It meant being in several hospitals, and I was much tried by my circumstances till assurance came from the Holy Scriptures that all would be well again. And so it was. But it was quite a test getting the medical and surgical people to agree to let me go again to the mission field. Finally, it had to be a blended decision from a tropical specialist who pronounced me as fit in everything physical but who would take no responsibility for my going because of my having had the spinal fracture. I returned to the last hospital I had been in, the Orthopaedic Hospital, London, where they had said that the Royal Infirmary, Edinburgh, had helped to give me a wonderful back, and that I had a spine like that of a snake! There at the Orthopaedic Hospital they again thoroughly examined and X-rayed my back, and showed me the negatives, saying that had the injury been more serious I could have been paralysed from the waist down, but that the fracture had healed 'as clean as a baby's skin.' For a time I had to prove that my back was well and strong, and I returned to the Orthopaedic Hospital for a further examination when I was told that my back

[181]

was stronger than ever. At my request they kindly gave me a letter for the Worldwide Evangelization Crusade, saying so, and that I was fit to return to the mission field. Since it was not private, I read it when I came out of the hospital, and it said, with what seemed to me, quite a flourish, 'and this man is fit to go to China!'

For three years Miss Annie Sandison from Cullivoe, Yell, Shetland Islands, and I had been engaged to be married, and soon after our wedding, a friend donated enough money for us to return to India. We did not go, for Norman and Pauline Grubb, leaders of the Worldwide Evangelization Crusade at that time, asked us to pray about staying with them at the Home Base and sharing in the work there. This we did, and had assurance that this was the will of the Lord for us. We stayed, and have been in varied jobs on the W.E.C. British Staff ever since. The money-gift was used up in various missionary ways.

At a missionary conference, a young man named Ronald Davies heard the late Rex Bavington and myself speak about the spiritual need of the peoples of Central Asia, and said that he knew that it was the will of the Lord Jesus that he should go to Baltistan as a messenger of the Gospel. His Bible training finished, he went there for a time and then to the North-West Frontier Province. He became a firm friend of ours, and, later on, of our young family who were all very fond of him.

Long and arduous were the journeys Ronald Davies made in Baltistan, and few who ever listened to him relate his experiences there will ever forget them. One of his stories was about the conversion to Christ of a dumb Balti. Ron, as we came to know him, had arrived in a village, and had gathered a number of men around him. Having cooked some food he invited them to share it with him. One and all, including one who was dumb, refused. They made it clear to Ron that they were Moslems and would not risk eating anything that might be unclean to them. Nothing daunted he got out some Bible pictures on canvas, and eagerly told them of the Bread of Life sent down from heaven. They listened, made a few comments and went away. But the dumb man returned, making signs that he would like to see the pictures again and have them explained to him. Out came the canvasses, and Ron, using signs as best he could, related to him the kindness of God our Saviour. The dumb man was all attention, and next day he was back again, and made once more his welcome request to see the pictures. Fixing on the one depicting Christ crucified he pointed to him upon the cross, then at his own breast, and then up to heaven. Next, he pointed to Ron, then at himself, and raised two fingers. They were two! Then he pointed to the Saviour on the cross and raised one finger signifying that he and Ron were one in Christ. He would eat with Ron. What joy there was in Ronald Davies as he told how the dumb Balti and he sat and ate together.

Transferred to the Afghan Frontier, it seems that Ron did not need to study the language much. It came naturally to him from his close and sympathetic life among the people in their homes and all around. Their terms of speech, inflections and mannerisms were adopted by him seemingly without a thought. One day, travelling by motor-lorry, and as usual, dressed in Frontier fashion, he joined heartily, as was his wont, in the lively conversation of his fellow passengers. They thought that he was a Pathan. But a mentally afflicted woman, listening intently, pointed a finger at him crying derisively 'He is a Sahib! He is a Sahib!' Men frowned at her saying, 'Never mind her. She is mad! She is mad!' The woman loudly insisted that Ron was a Britisher. He simply laughed, and was not asked to say either yea or nay about what he was.

Another day he was shamefully set upon in the bazaar, punched, kicked, and knocked to the ground, all without any retaliation on his part. Taken home, he recovered, and was soon back again in the same place having the same mind as the Apostle Paul at Lystra. Where our love is, there certainly is our life.

It was quite a common sight to see Ron surrounded by children. A missionary tells how, as he sat by the fire one evening, the door was gently pushed open, and a little Kashmiri girl, four years old, shyly looked in to say that she wanted to play with Lal Sahib (Red Sahib) so called because of his red hair and beard. He did not disappoint her, and their shouts of laughter and merriment were like those of the boys and girls playing in the streets of Jerusalem, now become the mountain of the Lord of Hosts, the Holy Mountain. Ron said that he thought that the children where he worked did not laugh enough. But this could not be said when he was with them. A fellow worker says that the last time she saw him he was sitting holding one of their little foundling children, and she was asking him to take her with him wherever he went. And Lal Sahib was always the friend of the old, and greatly loved by the old in return. Aziza, whom he sometimes playfully teased, and who walked with a stick with which she used to chase him, often looked back on these happy times and spoke of them with tears of joy. The more despised, tempted and downtrodden the people were, the more he loved them. Appreciating them he lifted them up whenever he could and always wanted to show them the power of the Lord Jesus, the Son of God, to save and to keep. He was their brother man. He cared for their condition, their interests and their souls. As it was prophetically said of his Lord and Master, 'Yea, he loved the people.'

From the Frontier, Ronald Davies came back to us in London for an operation and we all became accustomed to the tall red-bearded figure with the Indian sandals in our midst. The operation and the effects of it over, he went around the country speaking at meetings. All his bearing and appearance spoke of the East. There was no mistaking him for anyone else than a missionary from that part of the world. *En route* again for India, a friend from France and he travelled together as far as Paris, and she said to him that having enjoyed the hymn-singing by those who saw them away at the railway station, sometime she would like to hear them sing again. He shook his head saying that he did not want to return home again and that he would rather hear them sing when they were all gathered together in their heavenly Father's house. Nevertheless, it was our mutual happiness to be together many times later in worship and praise of the Christ who died for us.

Ron was busily engaged in his missionary service when war broke out in 1939, and he spoke of the bewilderment and struggles he had when he was called away to serve in the Indian Army. His Christian character there was often remarked on. Even the most stubborn had to acknowledge the loveliness of his life. Wherever he happened to be stationed, and someone was witnessing for Christ and Him crucified, Ron Davies was by his side with help and fellowship. One day in the Lucknow Soldiers' Home, he passed through the coffee-room where a University undergraduate was seated, a man of pronounced Unitarian views. As Ron Davies left the room he jumped up and said aloud to all with such moving sincerity, 'There goes a Christian!' Ron became a Major and served six years

[185]

in the Indian Army in Burma, Java and Sumatra, and was mentioned in despatches for bravery and devotion to duty, about which he would never speak. His pay was high, but he kept none of it for himself, giving instructions at his bank to give it to various missionary causes. When he came to the end of his army career he found that his giving had left him with a bank credit of about one shilling and a penny. Lal Sahib, or Khadim Masih (Servant of Christ), as he liked himself to be known, demonstrated in his life the beauty of his Lord and Master. There are those who say that they never heard him speak ill of anyone, and when he himself suffered from others who felt that his ways did not suit them, he was forgiving and loving. Khadim Masih appeared to be a man possessed with one passion, the Lord Jesus Christ. Love for him, love for humanity, and constant endeavour for the spread of the Gospel, were his life. Tall, strong, broad-shouldered, and of ruddy complexion he looked a Pathan from the wild regions of the North-West. Dressing as they did, it was his way to mingle among them, showing them the loving kindness of his Saviour in order to win them to him.

After the war we welcomed him back in Britain, and he spent that short leave eagerly urging young men and women not to fail in their high responsibility of going out to the unevangelised to preach Christ and the Gospel. But he was soon on the soil of India again and he lost no time in proceeding to Northern Kashmir where he had been appointed Field Leader. He was just where he wanted to be, back in the stretch of country which he knew so well, from Haripur in the North-West Frontier Province to Sopor by the Wular Lake, Kashmir. He was full of enthusiasm, and various plans were produced and talked over with other missionaries for the extension and intensifying of the work. A wooden building which had been given to him was to be brought down from the hills, and erected as a meeting-place. Christian workmen were to be found to put it up, and there were plans for evangelistic endeavours in other townships. But while they planned for peace there were those who were for war, and thousands of murdering Pathans were already staining with innocent blood the lovely vales of Kashmir.

A mission centre had been opened at Buniyar, and Lal Sahib went there to talk with the workers, and to see the house and the district. Over his inevitable and only luxury, a pot of tea, he discussed with the three ladies who were there, Margaret Brown, Lily Boal and Bessie Southall, plans for the future of the work; and they found him to be a more serious-minded and more responsible Ron than they had ever known him to be. Painstakingly he went into the question of their water supply, and all other matters concerning the lady missionaries' new home, connected with health and general welfare. Ron then left to go to the mission-base at Haripur.

For the ladies the days passed busily enough, but rumours of war came nearer and fiercer to them. But all with whom they spoke said that there was no danger to Christians. Pathans had entered the land to take revenge upon the Sikhs who had committed outrages farther south. But, then, these in their turn, had been retribution for massacres by the Pathans. So it was said, and said again! Lorries in great numbers and at alarming speed began to roll through Buniyar. They were loaded inside and outside, and even the roofs, running boards and bonnets were covered with Sikhs, men, women and children, bedding, cooking vessels and all kinds of belongings. Indian Army lorries, with grim-faced drivers, also thundered past, and the missionaries heard with horror that the Pathans had savagely won many fights, and were in rapid advance towards Buniyar, where Margaret Brown, Bessie Southall, Miriam Masih and her son, Mir Alum, and Misri Bano, and three little foundling girls, continued together in prayer. Lily Boal had gone to Srinagar.

Things were serious. Every horse-driven vehicle was loaded to breaking point with crowds of people, mostly Hindus, and driven away at the greatest possible speed. Soon after mid-day the lady-missionaries had remarked to each other that it would have been nice if Lal Sahib had been with them. About half an hour later a strong manly voice below their window enquired, in Urdu, if anyone was at home. Looking down they saw, with intense relief, the big, round, red face of Lal Sahib, and their anxiety departed in the joy of his smile. Ron had come! He was triumphing in his first and last test as a missionary field-leader. Looking back on that day Margaret Brown says they salute him with pride, pain and joy. The sight of blood-stained lorries in the town of Baramulla had sent him speeding to their rescue, in a pony-trap, secured at very high cost from twenty-four miles away. He was calm and re-assuring, and said that he was not concerned for himself but that he was for them, and that they were to take warm clothing and bedding, with some too for Lily whom they hoped to meet. A pony-trap has its limits, and they could not all get on to it. Lal Sahib said that Miriam, Mir Alum, and he, would follow on foot, sometime later. Off they went and Ron in all his simple greatness stood smiling, waving them goodbye.

Lily Boal had tried to get back to Buniyar but she was halted at Baramulla and not allowed to proceed any farther. Tribesmen had arrived and were looting and killing. She called at the R.C. Mission Hospital and the Sister at the gate said to her, 'You must come in, you are in great danger.' She went into the hospital. The wild men arrived and in a few minutes six people were killed and two seriously wounded. Everything was stolen from her by the Pathans who showed her their guns but said that they would not kill her, though time and again she expected to be shot or burned with everyone in the hospital, since all around was blazing. The six killed were quickly buried, though at first they could not find the body of the shot British lady. After two days they found it down a well where she had been flung. Her husband, a British officer, was shot dead, leaving three orphan boys. Indian planes bombed the tribesmen, and set the nearby match-factory on fire. This was almost too much for them, and they prayed all the more. A Britisher at the risk of his life reached them fom Srinagar. The tribesmen were driven back by Indian troops, and he worked hard to get the wounded to Rawalpindi, a hundred and sixty-five miles away. He went with them and reported their plight to British authorities who sent lorries to Baramulla for them, and one dark night they all set out for North India. Lily asked to be allowed to sit beside the Commandant in the first lorry and when they came to Buni-yar they stopped and she went to the Mission House. All was cold and silent, and she wept for her fellow-workers. Then on they travelled through the long dark night and reached safety. Lily Boal came back home on furlough bringing the three orphan boys to their grandparents in Edinburgh.

Miss Margaret Brown takes up the story, 'The little streams go laughing and splashing down into the great Jhelum whose long pine-clad gorges are so wild and beautiful, and high above tower the great mountains. From the footworn paths and narrow roads, the cliffs fall sheer away to the rushing waters booming through their canyon walls. In autumn, the stern mountain sides are a blaze of golden bush with here and there sprays of crimson creeper, and everywhere the lights and shadows of the pine forests. On that mellow autumn day this was the setting for two Christians, the one young, strong and full of the joy of life, the tide of the love of God at the full in him; the other, poor, frail and gentle in that same love, full of desire to please the Crucified. She had been but a few years before delivered by Christ Jesus from one of woman's sorest captivities, that of Islam. A widow and a mother, her life was greatly bound up with that of her two children, Bibi Jan, a fine little lass of ten years and Mir Alum, her big strong carpenter son of seventeen. He was to be with his mother on that hard and painful day. Ron Davies and Miriam Masih! They were our best.

At Uri the raiders were held up for a time, but, breaking through, they killed most of the gallant little force of the Indian Army, and swept on up the valley, a destroying tidal wave. Bands of them reached Buniyar, and there was a fierce fight between some of them and some Indian Army troops helped by a few villagers. The ferocity of the Pathans was appalling and about twenty people were killed.

It appears that Ron had set out with Miriam and Mir Alum hoping to get away to Sopor ahead of the advancing murderers. Usually, we went by boat, but, of course, such could not be had now, and their plan was to get across used paths. But they were too late! Miriam was not a good walker, and it seems that Ron carried her at times. They were caught by the Pathans, rudely questioned and roughly handled, and in spite of remonstrances from their own officer, they refused to hear any plea for them. They angrily offered Miriam her release if she would repeat the Qualima, the short, hard, uncompromising Moslem creed that, There is no God but Allah and Muhammed is his prophet. But she was silent. Fiercely, they urged her, fiendishly warning her of the dire consequences of refusal, while she stood trembling beside Ron. And he spoke for her, hoping for her life to be spared. 'She cannot say it,' he cried. 'She cannot say it! She is a Christian!' But all was of no avail. The light in the Pathan is darkness, and can be as jet black night when mercy and love are needed. The rifles were fiercely lifted, savagely levelled and fired, and Miriam fell dead. Her pale lips had not moved to save her life and so deny her Saviour. Before this simple soul and her shining testimony we privileged ones, nurtured since childhood in the faith of Christ, bow our heads and pray that we too may be found as faithful as she was if such an hour should come to us.

It seems that in a very few minutes Ron followed her. Buffeted savagely, he, who ever gave us the sense of being ready to be offered, was asked who he was, and if he was ready to die. He said that he was Ronald Davies, Khadim Masih, and that he was ready. Once more the rifles wildly cracked and Ron died beside Miriam. Wild wanton butchery continued, and Buniyar went up in flames. Mir Alum was given a safe passage to Pakistan. The Son of God walked with him in a burning fiery furnace. For him, 'The form of the fourth was like unto the Son of God.'

So Lal Sahib passed into the presence of his Saviour yielding up his life in ready willingness of love. For him, it was the thing to do on that little bridge, spanning the sparkling stream running into the Jhelum River. Just as Ronald Davies had given much, so did he give all.

The missionary task and call to it are ever with us, and with it the claim of the Redeemer upon us to dedicate ourselves completely to Him and to the preaching of the

Gospel to all mankind. The religions which we have spoken of in this book may seem to their adherents to be suitable to them and to their world, but in them is no hope of salvation. This comes only from God in the Person and work of his only begotten Son. Hinduism, Buddhism and Islam, in their old and newer forms, are all without the message of redemption. In all of their theologies, theosophies, and moral codes (incomparably different from the revealed moral law of God in Scripture) there is no Saviour. Regrets and repentances for sin there often are, with attendant panances, pilgrimages and trying austerities, yet the void remains. The revelation of a Redeemer worthy in his Person as an acceptable sacrifice for sin remains unknown. There are no Glad Tidings, no Evangel. How different is the position of the Christian! He can say with the Apostle John, 'We know that the Son of God is come, and hath given us an understanding, that we may know him that is true, and we are in him that is true, even in his Son Jesus Christ. This is the true God, and eternal life.'

Almost half a century has passed since I was privileged to serve the Gospel in the Karakoram and the Khyber. The day hastens when the redeemed shall come from the east and the west and the north and the south and be partakers of eternal glory. Until that time Christ, unlike His servants, retains the dew of His youth and we know that He will continue to go forth, 'Conquering and to conquer'!

Bibliography

Addison, James T., *The Christian Approach to the Moslem*, Columbia University Press, New York, 1942.

Ambedkar, B. R., *Pakistan or the Partition of India*, Bombay, 1946.

Anderson, J. N. D., *Islamic Law in the Modern World*, London, 1959.

Barker, Ralph, *The Last Blue Mountain*, Chatto and Windus, 1959.

Bauer, Paul, *The Siege of Nanga Parbat*, Rupert Hart-Davis, 1956.

Cragg, Kenneth, *The Call of the Minaret*, Oxford University Press, 1964.

Cable, Mildred, and French, Francesca, *Through Jade Gate and Central Asia*, Hodder and Stoughton, 1942.

Davidson, Flora M., *Hidden Highway*, Stirling Tract Enterprise, 1950.

Davidson, Flora M., *Wild Frontier*, Christian Literature Crusade.

Dods, Marcus, *Muhammed, Buddha and Christ*, Hodder and Stoughton, 1905.

Duff, Alexander, *Missions the Chief End of the Church*.

Gairdner, Temple, *The Reproach of Islam*, London, 1921.

Grousset, Rene, *In the Footsteps of the Buddha*, G. Routledge & Sons, London 1937.

MacLean, Fitzroy, *Back to Bokhara*, Jonathan Cape, 1959.

Marsh, Charles, *Share Your Faith With a Muslim*, Echoes of Service, London, 1975.

Bibliography

McClung, Floyd, *Just Off Chicken Street*, Fleming Revell & Co., New Jersey, U.S.A.

Muir, Sir William, *Sweet First Fruits*, The Religious Tract Society, London, 1913.

Nicolson, Angus, *A Guide to Islam*, Drummond Tract Enterprise, Stirling, 1951.

Padwick, Constance E., *Temple Gairdner of Cairo*, London, 1928.

Padwick, Constance E., *Muslim Devotions*, London, 1928.

Pallis, Marco, *Peaks and Lamas*, Cassell & Co., London, 1948.

Pennell, Alice M., *Pennell of the Afghan Frontier*, London, 1914.

Pierce, Bernard, *A Mountain Called Nun Kun*, Hodder and Stoughton, London, 1953.

Plymire, David V., *High Adventure in Tibet*, Gospel Publishing House, Springfield, Missourie, U.S.A.

Sale, George, *The Koran*, Many Editions.

Sadhu Sundar Singh, *Reality and Religion*, Macmillan & Co., London, 1924.

Smith, Harold F., *Outline of Hinduism*, The Epworth Press, London, 1934.

Streeter, Burnett Hillman, *The Buddha and the Christ*, Macmillan Co., 1932.

Tyndale-Biscoe of Kashmir, *Autobiography*, London, 1956.

Trotter, Lilias, *The Master of the Impossible*, London, 1938.

Walter, H. A., *The Ahmadiya Movement*, Humphrey Milford, Oxford University Press, London, 1918.

Wilson, J. Christy, *Apostle to Islam, Biography of Samuel M. Zwemer*, 1952. Grand Rapids, U.S.A.

Wilson, J. Christy, *The Christian Message to Islam*, New York, 1950.

Wolff, Joseph, *Narrative of a Mission to Bokhara*, 1848,
William Blackwood & Sons, Edinburgh and London.

Zwemer, Samuel M., *The Moslem Doctrine of God*, New
York, 1905.

Zwemer, Samuel M., *The Moslem Christ*, London, 1912.

Several of the above books give the titles of other interesting and edifying books.